DROPSHIPPING

How to Make $300/Day Passive Income, Make Money Online from Home with Amazon FBA, Shopify, E-Commerce, Affiliate Marketing, Blogging, Instagram, eBay, Retail Arbitrage, Social Media, and Facebook Advertising

By
James Ericson

TABLE OF CONTENTS

INTRODUCTION

I want to thank you for purchasing this book *Dropshipping: How to Make $300/Day Passive Income, Make Money Online from Home with Amazon FBA, Shopify, E-Commerce, Affiliate Marketing, Blogging, Instagram, eBay, Retail Arbitrage, Social Media, and Facebook Advertising.*

In this book, we will show you how to make money online with the help of many tools available in today's day and age. You have to remember that times are changing; more people are resorting to online shopping and buying digital products online. This means that there is more demand for people looking towards spending money when it comes to online products which also means that there are more opportunities for people looking to start an online business. With that being said, if you are looking to start making $300 a day from online businesses, then there is no better time to start it.

As this industry is new and growing, there is a lot of demand, and soon, it should be filled up. What we recommend is getting into these industries as quickly as possible. This way, you will have a better chance of starting a business and to flourish in this fantastic industry. In this book, we will talk about all the top online businesses you can get into to make money. Also, we will talk about the future of online businesses and how you can be one step ahead of your competition. This will allow you to have a long and prosperous business or businesses, so I hope you enjoy and take action on the information coming your way.

CHAPTER 1
The Basics Of Passive Income

Many people are claiming that they earn $1,000 up to $10,000 a month while working from home. Whereas, other people who work a day job, can't fathom the idea of working from home. You might be asking if it is really possible to make money online and for it to be passive. Plain and simple, yes, and there are many already generating millions. Nonetheless, you will have to learn the right knowledge and implement it before you can start making money. Once you have managed to learn the secrets, you can make money and tons of it. Once you are done reading this book, you will have all the tools you need to make $300 day easily. The results might be different from person to person. Some might make $100,000 the first month, and some might even lose money, but if you play your cards right, you should have no problem making heaps of cash. There are many people already making insane amounts of money from the comfort of their home, and the truth is you can, too. Listen, if you want to live your life on your own terms and want to make insane amounts of money, this book is definitely for you. If any of you are wondering if you can still make money online, then the answer is yes. 100%. Many are making money from these techniques already. You can be making millions of dollar sitting on a beach, and this isn't an exaggeration. Believe in yourself and get to work and you will be there in no time.

Why Make Money Online?

Earning money online is one of the best ways to earn passive income. It is also the kind of opportunity that will allow you to make a decent amount of income even if you just stay in the comfort of your home.

We live in the age of digital technology. It is the golden age of computers. People and businesses now begin to shift from physical to online transactions. In fact, every business these days almost always has some form of an online presence. Many people who are engaged in e-commerce are also on the rise. Indeed, many opportunities become available online. In fact, some people live solely from the profits that they make online. And, mind you, we are not just talking about a $1,000 income, but $100,000 and even higher. This is why so many people these days want to learn how to make money online effectively.

When you make money online, you are also able to minimize your cost. You do not need to rent an office space that costs hundreds of dollars a month. Instead, you can just set up your own domain space on the Internet which costs as low as less than $50 a year. Instead of being tied to a limited geographical location, you can send all your customers and would-be customers to your website regardless of their physical location. The whole world becomes your market.

Making money online is a new trend. Indeed, people are learning how they can take advantage of the online world to earn a decent income. There are those who successfully make a part-time income, and there are also those who work full time online. But don't think it is as easy as it seems. Indeed, there are also those who fail to generate even $20 when they tried to work online. This is why it is essential for you to build a strong foundation and develop your understanding.

Getting Started

Are you ready to make money online? If yes, then it is time for you to get prepared. When you work online, you can enjoy a good level of flexibility. However, this does not mean that you will only be working for a few hours. On the contrary, if you want to be truly successful, then you should give it as much time and effort as you can. However, if the best that you can do is to give it a few hours in a day, then that will also do but do not expect to be able to establish your business quickly if you do not give it enough time.

Making money online is like a business. As such, you can expect to have some starting capital. However, unlike the traditional business, you do not always need to have significant capital, depending on how you intend to make money. For example, when you make money by blogging, you will only need to have a good-quality computer, a blog domain of your own, and Internet access.

All these are very common these days. With respect to having your own URL, it only costs less than $30 a year. Of course, you can also decide to invest a considerable capital, for example, if you choose to invest in cryptocurrencies or trade options. Do not worry. We will discuss all this later in the book. For now, you just have to get ready. So, if it is not really money, what do you need to prepare? You will have to prepare for yourself. Making money online can be challenging in the beginning, especially if you are not that literate in using a computer. However, do not worry as you can learn all these things quickly. You just have to be patient and continue to do your best. For now, you need to be in the right mindset.

If you want to make money online, then you should always be willing to learn. The fact that you are reading this book is a good sign that you want to learn and that you are taking the right actions. Indeed, it is essential to put your knowledge into actual practice. After all, real learning is not just about knowing, but it is more about doing. This book will give you the insight, the keys that you need that can unlock the door to financial freedom; however, it is up to you to put your new-found knowledge into actual practice. Making money online also takes skill. You have to practice regularly. Do not worry; just keep on doing your best and remember that success is well within your reach. Let us now discuss the different ways that you can make money online.

Affiliate Marketing

Many people also earn the right amount of profits through affiliate marketing. This is where you promote other people's products, and you earn a profit on the time a sale is made through your affiliate link. Depending on the affiliate program that you have, you can also earn every time a person clicks on your affiliate link or for every page view. This will depend on the terms and conditions of the affiliate program.

You can message a business, and it may give you an affiliate link that you can use. Usually, people just join an affiliate network like Clickbank. This is the easiest way that you can jump into affiliate marketing. When you enter an affiliate network, you can choose among the different products. Your job is to market and sell your selected products. You can do this by writing something about what you are marketing, such as a product review or comparison, among others. Now, it is easy to have an affiliate link; the challenging part is having people to buy from your affiliate link. This will involve a combination of different things such as having a website, writing posts, promoting on social media, and others. You should also establish and tap your quality followers.

Just how much can you earn? This will depend on the price of the item that you are able to sell, as well as the agreed percentage of your share—your commission. Some online marketers excel at selling affordable products. The key is to sell a massive quantity so that you can earn a decent return. There are also those who like to sell only expensive products. All they need to do is to make one or a few sales a week to earn a decent income. Of course, you can promote both types of items if you want. The important thing is to make a sale so that you can earn a commission.

Although affiliate marketing seems simple, it is not that easy to do. For one, you will have to increase your visibility. This means having to work on your SEO. In order to gain the trust of your audience, you also need to come up with a presentable website or blog, among others. As you can see, there are many things that you need to do to establish yourself as a marketer. Indeed, this takes time, but it is also very much worth it. In fact, when it comes to making money online, successful marketers earn a very high income. It just really requires lots of work in the beginning, especially when you are still building your foundation.

Shopify and Other Online Stores

If you are interested in selling things, then you might want to try Shopify and other online stores like Amazon. These sites have millions of customers and visitors who are looking to spend their money on something. You merely have to sign up for a seller account, and you can start selling right away. Of course, you also have to read and observe specific terms and guidelines. The key here is to follow the number one principle of making a profit: buy low, sell high. If you want, you can even be the one to manufacture the products that you are going to sell.

It is noteworthy that there are now many people who do this kind of business, so you can expect to face some competition. Do not worry; competition is normal and even crucial in business. It only proves that there is indeed a market that has a high demand. This means that there is an opportunity for you to make money. If you want to take this route, be sure only to offer high-quality products. Remember that you are not looking for a one-time sale. Instead, you need to establish a continuous flow of income. Be mindful of the reviews that you get. This is why it is essential to only sell products that have good quality. If a buyer is not pleased with your product, there is a chance that he might write a bad review of the product. This is a sure way to discourage potential customers from buying from you.

You should also have a strong marketing arm. Even if you have excellent products to sell, you cannot make a good income if people do not even know that your business exists. This is why it is essential that you also work on your promotional strategies. These days, businesses usually rely on social media to spread the word about their business. We will talk more about how you can use social media effectively in the next chapter.

An online store can significantly cut down your expenses. You would not have to worry about paying office rent. In fact, you may not even need to hire any employees. And, since everything happens online, the store is also open 24 hours a day, round the clock. When you sell items online, remember that it is essential that you offer high-quality products and tap the right market.

Blogging

Blogging is probably the most common way to make money online. What is a blog? Well, a blog is like an online journal or diary that you get to share with the whole world. It is something that you write online, on your web blog, and then people get to read your posts. There are many kinds of blog. For example, if you want to talk about the places that you have visited, then you can write a travel blog. If you are into exercise and nutrition, you can create a health blog. If you are into the latest clothing trends, then you can manage a fashion blog. There is a blog for anything and everything. Okay, but how do you make money from your blog? Well, there are many ways to make money with your blog. One of the most usual ways people make money from blogging is by using ads. When you have a blog, you can have advertisements to appear on a portion of your blog. You can earn money every time a person clicks on the ad and/or per view. Some people earn a six-figure income just by blogging. Indeed, this can be a highly lucrative venture.

So, how do you get into blogging? Well, the first thing that you need to do is to have a place on the Internet where you can blog. Now, if you just want to test the water, you might want to start with a free website. You might want to check blogger (from Google) or Wordpress. They will give you a free sub-domain that you can use for blogging. However, if you have already decided to pursue a career as a blogger, then you should have your own website blog. This means that you should buy a domain name. For this purpose, you might want to try GoDaddy or NameCheap.

So, what should you blog about? People always say that you should blog about what is currently trending or popular. However, the problem here is that trends change. Instead of blogging about things that you do not even understand, this book suggests that you should blog about what you love. This way you can blog for a long time and appreciate your blog. Since you will blog about what you know, then you can come up with quality content. The problem with many bloggers is that they just want to earn money and blog about things they do not understand, and this leads to poor content quality. Do not worry; no matter what your interest may be, there is undoubtedly a market for you. Do not forget that the whole world is your market.

When you engage in blogging, you have to increase your visibility online. The best way to do this is to optimize your blog for the search engines. This is known as search engine optimization, commonly referred to simply as SEO. When it comes to SEO, it is essential that you learn to use keywords. Gone are the days when you can just use any keyword that you want. Today, you need to be more specific. For example, if you are blogging about gardening, do not just use "gardening" as your keyword. There are now countless articles online that use the word "gardening" many times. You need to be more specific. What is it about gardening that you want to talk about? For example, instead of just "gardening," you can use, "plants to grow during summer."

Another essential point to take note of is the use of long-tail keywords. Long-tail keywords are keywords composed of at least three words. When you use keywords in your blog posts and articles, make sure that your keywords are at least three words long. Also, avoid using generic words. It helps to be specific. However, do not get too specific to the point that nobody else would think of searching for those terms. Take note that the keywords that you use should be those that people type in the search bar when they surf the web.

To know the bests keywords to use, as well as the amount of traffic specific keywords received, you should use the Google Keyword Planner. Google Keyword Planner will not just show you the number of times particular keywords have been searched over a specified time, but it will also offer suggestions for the best keywords that you can use. To gain access to the keyword planner, you should sign up for an Adwords account from Google. Take that this is different from an Adsense account. Adsense is for allowing people to post relevant ads on your blog while Adwords will enable you to be the one to post advertisements for a fee.

Another thing to take note of is quality. No matter how much you promote your blog's visibility, it is still essential that you have exciting and high-quality content on your blog. In fact, it is the quality of your blog posts that will really draw people to your blog. Make sure that every post you make has a good quality.

Another effective way to earn from blogging is by selling an ebook on your blog. Some people do not like the idea of posting ads on their site or blog, and this is understandable. Although they do not make money from Adsense, they earn money by selling an ebook/ebooks on the blog. For example, if your blog is about yoga and you share interesting articles about yoga. If people like what you share and see that you are selling an ebook on yoga, then they will most likely buy that ebook. The articles on your blog will gain the trust of the readers which can then lead to a successful sale of your product.

So, is blogging for you? Well, if you are the type who loves to write and connect with people who share a common interest, then you should definitely try blogging. However, if you would rather keep things to yourself, then you might find it hard to adjust to being a blogger. But, do not be discouraged; being a successful blogger is something that you can learn. Put your heart into whatever it is that you are doing and always do your best.

With that note, we come to the end of this chapter. Remember, in the next chapters, we will show you exactly how to make money from the methods listed in this book, and this chapter was to brief you on what is to come.

CHAPTER 2
Drop-Shipping 101

Hopefully, you now have a clear idea of what drop-shipping is all about. In the previous chapter, we gave you a brief description of it. We will now further talk about it. Currently, there are two different types of drop-shipping. The first one is online drop-shipping, where you just send over the product to your customer from your supplier. Or the next one, where you buy the product in bulk, and you send it over to the companies' warehouse allowing you to drop-ship from there. There are many ways to drop-ship, so let's go into the details on how they all work.

Online drop-shipping
Online drop-shipping is one of the most common ways people decide to start up their drop-shipping business these days. This is the method which comes to mind when people talk about drop-shipping.In this method, you will have to find a supplier which can provide you with high-quality products at a cheap price. One thing you have to make sure about is that he or she will have to ship out the product for you directly to the buyer without you doing any of that. Using this method, you will most likely have to make your own website like using Shopify to make your online store, or if you don't want to create your site, you can use eBay. We will discuss more which websites to choose for your drop-shipping business later in this book.

Now, if you decide to use this method for your drop-shipping, you will have to make sure that you have a safe and secure way of collecting payments from your client. Not only will it help you get paid safely, but it will also make your customers feel safe once they decide to make a purchase on your website or product. If you are thinking about making your website for your products to sell, then make sure you add a trust badge on your site. If you use Shopify as your drop-shipping website, it will show trust badge in the footer menu of your site so don't worry about that if you're considering using Shopify to create your drop-shipping site. One more thing to remember, make sure you have a PayPal account. Most people will use PayPal to make purchases on your site, so if you want to get paid, you need to create a PayPal account.

Now, I want to discuss the benefits of using online drop-shipping for your business. Like I mentioned before, you don't have to hold any inventory. Meaning, there is no need to buy any products in bulk or rent out a warehouse where you can store your products. All you are just going to do is to make a website, upload the product on your site, and once someone purchases the product, you will merely give the shipping information to your supplier, and he or she will mail it out to them! Plain and simple. The only thing you might need investment would be buying a domain name for your website, which I highly recommended. The domain would cost you around $10 a year. Also, if don't do coding for a living, you might have to use a website platform to start selling your products and to collect payments which will cost you additionally $30 to $120 a month (depending on which website platform you decide to use, etc.) If you want, you can pay for the whole year with your website provider which will save you money.

Just like any business model, there are some flaws to this method, so let's talk about them. The main one I see is shipping times, and we live in a world where websites ship products in a day. Most of the times, the supplier you will be working with would be from China, so the orders for your clients will be shipped out from China. For you to actually make a profit on your sale, you will have to use the most cost efficient way of shipping, which will result in slower shipping times. Now, this isn't a total deal breaker, but people are impatient; some more than others.

So, if you don't pick the right supplier and shipping methods, you can expect to get refunds. Don't you worry, not all your orders will get refunded and I will also show you the best tricks and techniques to get fast delivery to your client using this drop-shipping method later in the book, but don't expect shipping times of a day like most big competitors offer as it won't be possible with this technique.

Another drawback or flaw with this business model is that you won't be able to tell the quality of the products which you're going to be selling. So, I would recommend you buy the product before you put it up on your online store. It will lower the risk of your products getting refunded for quality issues. One more thing you have to worry about is driving traffic to your product. Since you won't be affiliated with any big companies, you will have to drive traffic to your own website or storefront using paid advertisement.

Warehouse drop-shipping

This method is similar to online drop-shipping in some ways and different in others. This is a bit confusing so let me explain. This method is identical in the sense that you don't hold any inventory and you don't ship out the products. Where it's different compared to the online drop-shipping method is that you will have to buy a certain amount of products upfront. But the benefit of having products with you would be fast shipping, which will allow you to have fewer chances of refunds and have better customer satisfaction.

So, let me explain to you how warehouse drop-shipping works precisely. First thing to remember is that you will be selling your product on a website like Amazon, you can still use the warehouse drop-shipping method with your site but you will have to rent out a warehouse and shipping would be your responsibly. Companies like Amazon will let you store it in their warehouse and ship the products out for you, which is why it is recommended to work with a big company when doing a warehouse drop-shipping model. So how it works is you find a product for cheap or buy it from a warehouse in bulk then you will ship your inventory to the company's warehouse. Once that is done, you will sit back and see the profits in your bank account, and you don't have to worry about anything like customer service, making a website, or capturing a payment, nothing! The company will take care of everything for you.

But, the upfront investment to start this business model is higher than online drop-shipping. Let me break it down for you. Depending on the product and how much of it you buy, you are looking to spend $1,000 to $2,000 on your inventory. Companies also charge you to have a seller's account that will be around $39.99 or more depending on how many products you sell. Plus a fee for every product shipped. So, as you can see, there is quite a bit more upfront investment compared to the online drop-shipping method. Although this method has a significant upfront investment, it also has some positives to consider.

There are a lot of benefits with this drop-shipping method so let us talk about them. The best advantage of using this drop-shipping method is that you can actually quality check the products before you decide to sell your products. As you know by now, it is imperative that you check your products' quality before you ship them off for your refund rates to be low. Another great benefit with warehouse drop-shipping is that, once you have shipped it to the company's warehouse, you don't have to worry about anything else. The company will take care of the shipping, etc. Another huge benefit with this business model is that you will not have to worry about advertising your product as much as the online drop-shipping method since your product will be listed in the company's website which already gets a lot of traffic. You won't have to worry about promoting your product too much which could mean less paid advertisement and more money in your pocket.

All being said, there is one major flaw I see with this method of drop-shipping. The flaw I see is that there is no guarantee all your products will sell if any. Even though you will be listing your product on a website which gets a lot of traffic, it won't always equate to sales. Remember, there will be a lot of products you will be competing with on the website, so making sure your product sells is crucial if you don't want to lose your investment.

So hopefully, you now know what drop-shipping is and the different ways you can go about starting your drop-shipping business. If you're still confused, then don't worry and keep reading. It will begin to get less confusing as we go along in this book, and hopefully, everyone reading this book now has an understanding of what it takes to start a drop-shipping business. Trust me, drop-shipping is one of the most straightforward business models to scale up and make money on so keep on reading as we will now show you how to start your very own store.

Shopify

For people who don't know what Shopify is, Shopify is an e-commerce company founded in Canada. What Shopify provides is an e-commerce platform or an online store for its users. It was initially established by Scott Lake, Daniel Weinard, and the current CEO, Tobias Lutke. Essentially, what Shopify provides you with is a secure online store where you can sell products to customers online. Most people use this website for online drop-shipping rather than warehouse drop-shipping since Shopify does not provide users with a warehouse. That being said, starting your very own drop-shipping business using Shopify as your platform is straightforward and cost-effective compared to other platforms.

To start making money with drop-shipping using Shopify as your platform, you will need is a supplier, which can ship out the products anywhere in the world for cheap. That's it for the requirements. Now, I want to get specific with a start-up cost of getting started with Shopify as it is not free, but it is really cost-efficient compared to other business models out there.

Now, first things first, you will need to buy a domain name. You really need to make sure that you're website looks legit, and for that to happen, you will need a domain name. Buying a domain name is inexpensive. It will only cost you around $11 to $18 USD per year, depending on the domain name. Now, once you get that sorted, you will now have to sign up on Shopify, and sinceShopify offers a free 14-day trial, I would recommend that you make sure that the store name or brand you come up with is not taken before you buy a domain name for your website or store. Once you have decided your store name, etc., it will now be the time to buy a package from Shopify which will allow you to start selling your products. Shopify offers three packages, which include

- Basic Shopify package ($29.99 USD) a month
- Shopify package ($79.99 USD) a month
- Advanced Shopify package ($299.99 USD) a month

Also to note, if you want to save money, you can buy these packages upfront on a yearly basis. But that's totally up to you.

Now, you might be wondering which one to get started with? Well, let me explain each of them to you. If you're just starting your drop-shipping business, I would like to say right off the bat that you don't need the advanced Shopify package. Once you have your business rolling and if you want to expand, you can do your research on it and upgrade. But for starters, just pick between the basic Shopify package and the Shopify package. If your funds are low, and you want to start making money online, then you can start off with the basic package, but if you have some extra cash to spare, then I would recommend upgrading to the Shopify package as it has some useful benefits.

The valuable benefits this Shopify package provides you with compared to the basic Shopify package is the lower amount of online credit card rates compared to the basic Shopify package. Even though it is minuscule, it adds up once you start making over thousands of dollars a month. Another great benefit of using Shopify package compared to basic Shopify package is that you can start making your own gift cards. As you know, in order to make sales on this platform, you will need to get some traffic first before you can actually make some sales online. So, having these small incentives can add up to more sales in the future. Other than that, these packages are identical. If you are using Shopify for online drop-shipping purposes, you can go with either package which fits your budget. Now, it's up to you which one you want to get started with.

One more thing you can invest in to really make your store stand out is logos, and you will need a logo for your Shopify store. You can get it done professionally by hiring someone on fiverr.com. The logo will not cost you more than $25 USD to get started. One thing to note, you do not need to hire someone to make your logo. It can be quickly done for free by using canva.com to create your free logo. But regardless, free or not free, you will need a logo.

To sum up the total costs of getting started with drop-shipping using Shopify.

- Shopify package $29.99 or $79.99 USD
- Domain name $ 11 to $18 USD

- Logo $0.00 to $25.

So, to get started with Shopify, it will cost you $40.99 + $29.99 USD every month after that and if you go for the cheapest option or $122.99 + $79.99 every month after that. Regardless, the startup should be quite affordable for anyone.

Now, let's talk about the work you will have to put in for your Shopify business to flourish. You will have to make sure your website looks presentable. Now, Shopify provides you with some great themes which can be used to build up your site. But it does require some work to be put in. Another thing you will have to take care of is customer inquiries and complaints. Since it is your brand and company, you will have to deal with everything from complaints to fulfilling an order. So, make sure you have an email created for your store inquiries. Also, as I said before, you will have to emphasize more on getting traffic since no will know about your store except your family and friends. Other than that, you should be fine.

How you get paid on Shopify is simple as well. All you have to do is make a PayPal account since some people might choose to complete their transaction using PayPal. Also, Shopify will make you put in your banking information. So, for the others who use a credit card to make a purchase on your store, Shopify will directly deposit into your account.

The final thing I would like to discuss is how much you can really make using Shopify and online drop-shipping method. Since it is your brand and your company, you can make as much as you want. You can become a millionaire or a billionaire with this method, as long as you build a following for your business, which again, will be talked about in the later chapters. Overall, the sky's the limit! Work hard and be patient; you will get what you desire.

Amazon FBA

If you have been living under a rock, Amazon is one of the biggest e-commerce companies in the world with its founder and owner's net worth is a whopping 150 billion dollars, making him the richest man in the world. Jeff Bezos founded his company in the early 90s, and his goal was to sell books online. Now, Amazon sells everything you can think off. Amazon is the biggest e-commerce company in the world, and its website has one of the highest amounts of online traffic in the world. Needless to say, working with Amazon could make you money.

Now, you might be wondering, what does the FBA stand for? It stands for Fulfillment by Amazon. What you have to do in order to a part of this program is simple, first find a product which you can get for cheap. Second, buy them in bulk, and finally, the third is to ship it to Amazon's warehouse where it can be shipped off to the customer. It is that simple. Now, with that being said, the startup cost with this business model is a little bit higher, so let's break it down.

Buying products in bulk for cheap will cost from $1000 to $3000 USD. If you sell more than 40 items a month, you will have to pay $39.99.

So, on the lower end, you can get started for $1000 USD to $3000 USD plus $39.99 a month if you sell more than 40 products. Plus, there is a charge for each product they ship out, but don't worry, it will only be charged once someone orders a product.

Even though there is a more significant upfront investment in this type of drop-shipping, it still has some benefits like, for example, since your products will be listed on Amazon, you will already be getting free traffic, which would equal higher chances of a sale. Unlike Shopify, Amazon takes care of the back ends like customer refunds, questions, etc. All you do is get the product, ship it to Amazon's warehouse, and you will start earning money.

Now, let's talk about the work you will have to do in order to get this business started from the ground up. The first thing is finding a cheap supplier. For you to actually make some profits, you will have to find products at a cost. Second, buy it in bulk, and third, ship it to Amazon's warehouse. When a business takes off, all you will have to worry about is restocking your products by shipping it to Amazon, so you can make more money. That's all the work you will have to do. As I said, all the back-end stuff, Amazon would take care of such as shipping, customer service, etc.

So, let us talk about how you will get paid on Amazon FBA. It is simple and similar to Shopify. You will first have to make a seller's account on Amazon. Once that is done, you will add your banking information to the account. Amazon will pay you the profits you made right into your bank account, and you don't have to worry about anything else, besides filing your taxes.

The final thing I would like to talk about is income, how much you can make on Amazon FBA. Since Amazon FBA is not a personal brand which you can grow, the revenue will be limited. I know the top earners can produce over two million a year using Amazon FBA. Which for some can be amazing to see this kind of cash. But for others who really want to build their brand, Amazon FBA would not be the answer. Now, the benefit with this business model is that if you do everything right, you can make money faster and could scale up higher. But there is a tap on the amount of money you can make here.

This should now help you really decide which business model you want to try out for yourself. Remember, you can easily make $300 a day with both of these models. Just remember, it takes hard work and the right knowledge. After this chapter, you should be on the right track to becoming successful in either of these business models.

CHAPTER 3
How To Be Successful In Drop-Shipping

Hopefully, by now, you have decided on which type of drop-shipping method and which website you will be moving forward with. Regardless of whichever method you choose, you will need to make sure that your products sell for you to actually make money. So, how will you actually sell products? Well, simply by finding a niche which already has customers and not enough products for all. Here's the cold truth, you will not sell anything or make any money if what you're selling does not have a demand for it. This is why choosing the right niche is imperative for your success in drop-shipping business.

Now, most of you might be wondering what a niche is. Well, to explain it in the simplest manner, a niche is something relating to or being a part of a certain product or service, etc. So, for example, selling something like a dog bracelet to dog lovers would be considered a niche. So, as you can see, having a niche to sell in is imperative for your success in this drop-shipping business. So, in this chapter, what I really want to talk about is how you can find a profitable niche where you can make some amazing profits without wasting money on buying your products in bulk and letting it sit in the warehouse or paying monthly fees and spending money on an advertisement without seeing any profits.

So, from my experience with Amazon, Shopify, and eBay, when you first initially start you won't be able to make a lot of money in niches which are saturated or have a lot of products to sell. Our goal is to get started with minimal money and slowly scale up. The ideal situation for you to make money is to be a bigger fish in a small pond rather than a smaller fish in a big pond. Your job is to find a profitable niche which hasn't been tapped into but you know it has the potential to sell and make you money.

So, to find out a niche which will actually sell and make you money, I have created two ways, or rather I should say, two techniques to find a niche and make money online. So, let me first show the websites I use to find a niche which will actually help you make money. The first website I use is Amazon. It is one of the biggest e-commerce websites. So anything that sells well on Amazon will sell anywhere. The second one is Facebook groups and Instagram pages. To find out what you could sell online on these pages will help you tremendously. Now, let's go into the depths of each way to find a profitable niche. We will begin with Amazon.

Amazon

As we know by now, Amazon is the biggest online store right now. So whatever sells in Amazon sells anywhere. So, if your goal is to find a niche which will make you money and is profitable, then you need to review Amazon's products.

If you have been to Amazon's website to purchase a product or anything of that matter, you will see the bestsellers rank under the product description. What that bestseller ranks symbolized is how much the product is being bought. This is very important for you to note. If the product is not selling on Amazon, which is the biggest e-commerce store in the world, it will not sell anywhere. Now, here is what you are going to do in order to find a product that sells.

The most essential thing you are going to do is get on your computer and go to Amazon's website. Now,what I want you to do is to go on to the bestsellers page on Amazon. This page will give you a rough idea on what sells and what doesn't. It also will show you niche products which are selling already. Anything in Amazon's bestseller's page will most likely sell, that is if you can offer it at a cheaper price. Regardless of which platform you will be using for your drop-shipping business, if Amazon has the same product for sale as you do, it will have it for the same price or cheaper than you would. This is the case most of the time, but if you can sell it for cheaper than your competitors then you have a winning product! Congrats.

Now, if that's not the case, it is about time to find an untapped niche. So go to the bestsellers' page on Amazon and look at the top 100 on that list carefully. If you see similar products from the same niche, then this niche is profitable. But it could be hard to penetrate into that specific market or niche. This is where we find a microniche. So for example, if the niche is iPhone accessories and there are multiple iPhone accessories on the bestseller list, what we will do is search up iPhone accessories on Amazon search bar. Then, we will go through the top six products and check to see their best sellers list. If the bestseller list showcases a number below 50, 000 for all six items, then this niche is profitable.

Hypothetically, you can sell in this niche and make some great profits. But if the competition is high, then there are fewer chances of you actually making profits. So, if you want to make sure the competition is low, look at the search engine number. If the search engine number has a number less than 5,000 items, then the niche is small and if the top six products have a ranking of lower than 50,000 on the best sellers rank, then you have a winning product and a niche to get into. So, if you search up iPhone accessories and it has 20,000 items for sale, it would be harder for you to tap into. On the other hand, if you search up iPhone phone cases and it has lower than 5,000 items for sale and the top six items best seller rank is lower than 50,000, we have a winner at hand. So this is how you use Amazon to find a profitable niche.

Facebook groups and Instagram pages

This is another place where you can find niches to sell. A lot of Facebook pages and Instagram pages are made to share videos and contents online for people to look at simply because they are a big fan of it. They have a special connection to this niche for some reason. It could be personal, business, who knows. But you can use this fan page or groups to offer them something they can't refuse.

Think about it, if you are a big fan of dogs and you loved dogs, wouldn't you want to buy a $25 t-shirt which says I love dogs? Of course, you would because you are a super-fan. Now, the best part about this method is that the people you will advertise your product to will most likely buy it, and there are a lot of pages online where there is a big following but no products to sell. So, in order to find these pages, all you have to do is search and think outside the box, as there are some pages waiting to be sold I love "something" t-shirt. So, look around and search and once you find your niche, you will be making some serious profits.

With that being said, let me share with you some niches which have made me money in the past.

- Dog lovers
- Cat lovers
- Lion lovers
- Car lovers
- Electronic accessories

These niches are still quite profitable, so do your research and if you like, then sell items from these specific niches.

Supplier

Finding the right supplier or the right wholesalers for your drop-shipping business is imperative, meaning that you can't "cheap out" or not care about this aspect. As you can imagine, your business will revolve around your supplier quite heavily. Truth be told, if you don't have any products that you can sell, then it would honestly be impossible for you to make any money which would therefore equal to no profits. Whereas, if you decide to "cheap out" and sell low-quality products, chances are people will return the products. Even though we discussed the importance of finding a proper niche to the importance of advertising the product the right way etc., it can't be overridden by an unreliable or a cheap low-quality product.

Finding the right supplier for your drop-shipping business purposes is imperative, for both quality purposes and shipping purposes. Now, if you are going to be using Amazon FBA or a similar type of drop-shipping method, then shipping times do matter in order for you to stock up your products, but it isn't the biggest of the deal for that drop-shipping model compared to drop-shipping methods using Shopify. Now with all that being said, quality is the biggest factor you have to worry about when selling your products. So, today, we will go through the top websites from where you can find great suppliers for your business. We will also talk about how to build a great relationship with them. And finally, for everyone using the method online-drop shipping, I will reveal a secret to getting the fastest shipping anywhere in the world so your customers stay happy and fewer refunds are being made.

We will break this chapter into two phases. First, we will talk about how to find suppliers for people using online drop-shipping. We will go through everything from finding the product, building a relationship with the seller, getting it shipped fast, and of course, making sure the product is of high quality. Then we will talk about finding a supplier or a wholesaler for warehouse drop-shipping method.

Online Drop-Shipping

So, finding a supplier for people using online drop-shipping as their business model could be challenging. Since most of the time, you will be going by assumptions, what your job with this process is to take out as much of the guesswork as we can and find the winning supplier which we are looking for. Now, there are a lot of websites online where you can find products for cheap. But from my experience, AliExpress has one of the best quality products and shipping times. If you have been doing some research online, you might have heard things like "AliExpress is dead" or things of that nature. But I am here to tell you that Ali Express still works amazingly and will help you make some serious profits online. There are some tips and techniques you need to know before you fully start using AliExpress as your sole supplier.

Now, if you don't know what Ali Express is then let me clarify it for you. Think of Ali Express as the Amazon of China. There are a lot of people selling products online on this website, mostly from China and as we know most of the products are manufactured in China. This means that the mark up on the products would be a lot less. Meaning you can easily sell it online for a higher price in the North American market, and to make things even better, the products on AliExpress are mostly similar types of products which are sold or are popular in the North American market. The point I am trying to make is this, people selling on AliExpress are selling it to people specifically who want to start their drop-shipping business.

There are some guidelines you need to follow before you start to use AliExpress to drop-ship products from, as there are some flaws. The things we need to look into before we start selling products using AliExpress are as follows:

- Suppliers review
- Product photos and description
- Epacket
- How many orders sold

Now, if all these points are checked out, then your supplier is good. So, let's begin with the supplier review. To find out if the supplier is good, the first thing you will need to do is check the reviews. Make sure the review on his or her store is at least 95% positive. If that's not the case, then either the product's quality isn't good or the product is something else when it gets delivered. Another thing to worry about is photos and the description. If the product has great photos and description, then most of the time, it shows that the seller actually cares about what he or she is doing and will do whatever it takes to keep his customers happy.

 Another thing to take care of is shipping. If the seller offers a shipping method known as e-packet, then the shipping times would be a lot faster than other suppliers. Normally, epacket delivers the product in 2-3 weeks, which are the fastest shipping times you will get on AliExpress. So, make sure your supplier provides you with e-packet. Also, to make sure this supplier is reliable, check out how many orders he/she has had. If it is higher than 500 orders, then they are in the clear. If all the points I just described to you are checked out, then the supplier is a good supplier and you can truly start to grow your business with him or her. And if the supplier doesn't check out on all these points, then find a new one.

One more tip I would share with you is that Ali Express tends to take some time when processing a payment. It could take up to three days. It is done simply for their security. If you want to expedite the process of processing the payment for your order to be shipped even faster, then I would recommend using Ali pocket.

Ali pocket is similar to a gift card. It is like a safe credit card for Ali Express. So, if you buy Ali pocket in bulk and use it to buy the product which you will be shipping it out to your client, then there would be no time to waste for processing payment and the order would be shipped right away.

Now, AliExpress is great for selling new trending stuff. But if your goal is to sell fan t-shirts and things of that nature then, it might not be the right choice for you. AliExpress has a lot of things to sell online, but the products it sells are not specific to niches and people. This is where print-on-demand t-shirts come in.

What is print-on-demand, you might ask? Well, print-on-demand is a service where you come up with a logo. Pick out a plain t-shirt sweater or whatever they have, and then what will happen is that the company will use your logo, put it on a t-shirt, etc., and directly ship it out to the customer or the buyer. That is what print-on-demand is. Now, there are a lot of websites to choose from. But the one I highly recommend is Pillow Profits. It is amazing. Not only do they have your good old t-shirts but they also offer things like pillowcases, shower curtain, or bed sheets which can be sent to a customer with your logo on any of those things.

Now, print-on-demand is ideal for those super-niche fan pages we talked about before. Since those fan pages are unique and hard to find, you need to be really unique with your products just like the page you are promoting it to. So, if your store is based on super-niche products, then it would be hard to find products on AliExpress and this is where Print-on-demand comes in.

Print-on-demand will offer you cheap supplies with whatever you want on it and fast shipping. Most of the print-on-demand websites have a really fast delivery since most of them are based in the United States, so you don't need to worry about shipping or any of that. Just make sure to pick out a print-on-demand website you like and come up with a logo.

Let's talk about building relationships with your suppliers. It is imperative that you build a great relationship with your supplier. Not only will it help you make more profits, but it will also help you get faster shipping times. What I am about to tell you applies more so to Ali Express rather than print-on-demand websites. Regardless of which website it is, you need a great relationship with your supplier. So, in order to build great relationships with your suppliers, here are the ways you can do so.

- Give them business
- Be accepting
- Leave them great reviews

So, giving them business is quite self-explanatory. If you want to build a great relationship, you have to give them business. You can't expect to be their "special customer" if you don't buy anything from them. So, make sure you first buy at least 20-25 items before you can think about asking them for a discount on your products. Another thing to be mindful about is making sure you don't get angry at them for a shipment which is a couple of days late or things of that nature. You have to remember that they are trying their best to keep you happy, just like you are trying to keep your customers happy. So make sure you are accepting and not making a big deal about small things like these. The final thing is to leave a positive review because let's face it, everyone cares about positive reviews. If you follow all these steps, you will start to build a great relationship with your supplier and you can slowly start to ask for things like discounts on your orders which would mean a higher profit margin for you. So make sure you start to build a great relationship with them.

With all that said, that is all for finding a supplier for people using online drop-shipping, let's talk about finding suppliers for people using Amazon FBA or warehouse drop-shipping. It is a little bit different but shares some of the same principles.

Warehouse drop-shipping

To find suppliers or products for this type of drop-shipping is a little bit easier compared to online drop-shipping. Since you can inspect all the product before you start selling makes it one step easier compared to the others. So, in short, there are three ways you can go about finding a supplier. The first one is using sites like

Ali Express, the second one is to find a warehouse where they are selling the products for cheap, and finally, buy products on special sales and re-sell them.

Now, you already know how to find the right supplier on AliExpress, but let's talk about how you can use AliExpress for warehouse drop-shipping. So right off the bat, once you find a product that you would like to sell, I would highly recommend you buy one of the products and really check it's quality. Once you have checked it out and made sure that the quality is of a high caliber, then you should contact the supplier and work out a deal. You see, since you will be buying the product in bulk, there would be higher chances of you actually getting it for a further discounted price, so make sure you ask for it so you can make even more profit. Finally, once that is all done, ship it to the warehouse and start selling.

That was using AliExpress. Now, let's talk about using warehouse or special sales to find your supplies. People don't realize that there are a lot of warehouses like Costco where you can buy stuff for cheap and sell it on Amazon. So, the way this process works is simple. Go to a warehouse like Costco, find a product in bulk for really cheap, and then transport it to Amazon's warehouse and start selling. Trust me, I have found so many cheap products on Costco for sale which have made me some great profits! Make sure you find these products and start selling them on Amazon.

Finally, one of the ways I have made tremendous amounts of money on Amazon FBA is by waiting for sales like Black Friday and things of that nature. I would buy products on sale for 50% to 70% off, and after the sale is done, I would sell it on Amazon at its original price. Although this method is not as frequently occurring as the other two, it will yield you a lot of profits so make sure you wait for these sales to make some real cash.

Finally, one secret method I have used before is finding listings on Craigslist and Facebook market places for products and supplies. Most of the times, you will find brand new stuff for sale near you, and the seller would be selling it off for next to nothing. So this would be your time to shine, find something in bulk for really cheap on these websites, work out a deal and sell it off on Amazon for a great profit. Now, if you found something for cheap but the quantity is low, then I would recommend using eBay to sell it on. I remember finding a brand new iPhone for super cheap. So, just like anyone else would do, I bought it and sold it off on eBay for a great profit. So, whatever you can find on these websites for cheap, make sure to act on them as soon as possible before they are gone.

With that note, we come to a conclusion of this chapter. I hope it was quite informative as we went thru a ton. We showed you how to find products the right way and where to source it from. This will allow you to become very successful in your business. Remember, if you follow the steps in this book, then you will be in a very good place when it comes to making money with this business.

CHAPTER 4
How To Market Your Drop-Shipping Store

By now, this book has been through everything regarding drop-shipping from the different types of drop-shipping businesses, how to start your own drop-shipping business, and how to pick out the most profitable niche and products. You see, everything is essential for your business to flourish, but if you can't get people to come into your page/website or to drive traffic to it, then nothing in this book will help you get sales. It's simple if no one is there to see your product or what you're selling, then no one is going to buy your products. It's just going to sit there and do nothing. So for you to make sales, you need to drive some traffic to your store or page, and that is what we will be talking about in this chapter; how to drive traffic to your store or page.

Learning how to drive traffic can be a challenging task. There is no right or wrong answer in this method. For some people, using websites like Facebook and Instagram could work amazingly, and that is all they do to drive traffic, whereas, for other's using free traffic techniques could be working beautifully making them some serious sales. So, it is more so of trial and error than getting it right in the first place.

When I started my drop-shipping business, I tried everything from Facebook ads to free traffic techniques like creating blogs and sending out emails. But all my drop-shipping businesses work differently, and sometimes, one business would work great on getting Facebook traffic and only that while others might work great on blogs traffic or emails, so it really just depends. For you to find out what works and what doesn't, you need to try it out and see for yourself. There is no way to tell if a specific add will generate you millions of dollars or not.

We will talk about the three most significant ways to drive traffic to your product page or website, which would be Facebook ads, Instagram shout outs, and finally, free traffic utilizing blogs, emails, etc. Try all of them out before you knock on one or the other. Like I said before, some might work beautifully for you compared to the others to make you try them out completely. With all that being said, let's tackle the hardest one first, Facebook.

Facebook

Facebook has a lot of users, over 2 billion of them to be exact. There are a lot of people on Facebook who would be interested in buying your products. The Facebook advertisement has been used by almost every drop-shipper you can find to drive traffic and this method is probably the cheapest and the most effective way you can use to drive traffic to your product page or store. Now, there are some steps you need to go through before you start advertising your product the right way in utilizing Facebook, which we will be going through this chapter.

First things first, when you create your Facebook ads account, you will need to make sure you add your website pixel on it. This is more important for people using the online drop-shipping method. Here is the thing. If you don't add your store pixel onto your Facebook ads account, it will not be able to collect data for your website and products. The pixel will receive things like what kind of people are checking out your product page and what kind of people are actually purchasing your product which would equal to a better ad campaign in future, as you would be able to target specific people to your product page or website. Now, after you have created your Facebook ads account and added your pixel to your Facebook ads account, we can now start to advertise your products. Here is what we need to take care of before we start advertising on Facebook.

- Finding products like yours
- Finding big companies' Facebook ads
- Targeting to a particular age group and country
- Amazing product photos
- Amazing caption
- Split testing

I know that there are a lot of things to worry about. But believe it or not, these are just the basics we need to take care of as there are a lot of other advertising methods which can be used. But for now, worry about the basics.

So, let's start off with the first step. Finding a similar product to yours on Google is essential to look for, as most of the times, it will show you the top sellers of your niche. When you start your Facebook ads campaign, it will ask you ad pages or companies related to your niche. What our job is quite simple, yet important. The first thing we will do is go online and search up our product. For example, if I am selling a car, I will look up "cars for sale," then I want you to click on all the websites which sell your products. So, in this hypothetical scenario, I would be clicking through Honda, Toyota, etc., so after you do that, I want you to write down all the websites which are related to your niche or product that you are going to be selling.

After you have written all the top websites, I want you to log into Facebook, then after that is done, I want you to search up the sites' Facebook pages. Once you have gotten that done, check to see if their Facebook likes are over 500,000 and if so, you have found a winner. You see, what Facebook does with that information on your campaign is that it will promote your product to the specific people on that page. So, let us get back to my hypothetical scenario. If I am selling a car and I add Honda to my targeted Facebook advertisement, it will then specifically target people who are interested in Honda. So, find a product and Facebook page which has over 500k followers, and then advertise the product to the people involved in that page.

Now that you have the keywords and the specific people you will be advertising your products to, it is now time to create an eye-catching advertisement. Since most of you haven't created a Facebook advertisement I assume, so in order for you to make sure your publication converts into sales, you will need to make sure your ads look good. Now, there are many tips and techniques out there spilled out by "supposedly" drop-shipping gurus, but some of you might have heard the phrase "if it ain't broke don't fix it" meaning that if there are big companies advertising their products successfully then there is no need to come up with your own unique way of doing it, as that trial and error could hurt your wallet.

If you did your research and tried to find big websites or companies specific to your niche, then there is a high chance that you might have seen their Facebook ads pop-up. The next time you see it, I want you to examine their advertising and see what kind of videos or images they are using. This will help you build your own advertisement, so make sure you review the ads and copy what they are doing. Trust me; it will work a lot better than you create your own special one.

Let's talk about finding age groups and country for your advertisements. If you know what your product provides to consumers, you would know what kind of people would be interested in purchasing your products. Before you start your first campaign on Facebook, it will ask you to put an age range on your advertisement. So, if you are going to be selling a car like I am, then I would probably set the age range around 25 to 65 as most of the people. Since most 18-year-olds won't be buying one by themselves and anyone over 65 won't either. So our goal is to target it to people who are most likely to buy your product. So, this takes some research and guesswork involved, but if you really specify the age, you will save the right amount of money and get more sales.

Whereas, for picking out the county or region to advertise it to, I would recommend you advertise it to the U.S.A only if your budget is small. Most of your buyers will be coming from the United States so no need to worry about advertising it to any other people. Now if you have some spare change left over, then you can further your audience to Canada which could get you more views and get you more sales.

After you have done all of this research, it is now time to create your advertising image and caption. People don't realize how important it is for you to have the right image and caption for your post. This will either make your post or break it. So, picking out the right photo and caption is imperative for your advertisement to be a success. Now, how do you pick out the right image for your advertisement? Simple, if you did your research correctly looking up big companies websites, then you would know the specific type of photo or caption to use, so mimic their advertisement.

Now, after you have decided upon the photos and captions you will be going with, it is now time to add a picture to your campaign. Two things to remember are to make sure the photo is high-definition. If it's not high-definition, then it won't stand out from the crowd, and it would also look unprofessional. Also, make sure the picture is compatible with smartphones advertisement. For you to check out what it would look like on a smartphone, just click on the smartphone advertisement option. It will show you what it looks like.

Now, let's talk about the caption. In order for you to get people clicking on the caption, you need to make sure that it is also eye-catching. For you to deliver that, you need to make sure you offer your clients with some incentives, like get this now for 50% off or only 50 in stock. Just like the big companies, you will need to make sure you create urgency by adding an incentive.

Finally, when everything is good to go and ready to be launched, you will utilize a tool called split testing. What you have to do is create two similar advertising campaigns with slight changes. For example, one ad could have an age group of 18-50 and the other 25-65. After the add has been running for some time, it will show you which one works better compared to the other, and this will help you optimize your ad campaigns in the future. This is optional but highly recommended.

That is all for Facebook advertising. Let's now talk about Instagram influencer advertising.

Instagram

Instagram is a great place to market your products and they have an enormous number of users, and most of the time, they are more engaging as compared to Facebook. So, if you are thinking about dismissing the idea of advertising on Instagram, think again as you would be leaving a lot on the table. Note that advertising from Facebook does go on onto Instagram, but it isn't as potent as it should be. So, when advertising on Instagram, we use a method called "Instagram influencer." It is quite simple. First, you will find an Instagram page which is related to your topic. Second, you will ask them to promote your product on their Instagram page and finally see sales come in. I have used a lot of methods, but this one always works! If you want quick sales on your Instagram account, use this method. Now, let's talk about the things you need to worry about before you start advertising on Instagram.

- Find the right influencer
- Make sure they don't have any BOTs
- Engagement

So, here is the thing for you to make sales and rack up some reasonable amount of cash from your sales. You need to make sure that your influencer would have the right audience. Meaning you cannot expect to make sales off of a dog bracelet if the page is about "I hate dogs." Do you see what I am trying to say? Make sure the product you are trying to sell is related to the people who are on that specific page. So, for example, if I want to sell a fishing rod, I would look up I love fishing pages to promote on that.

Now, before you go out finding your influencer page, you need to make sure that the page has at least 300k followers. If it doesn't, then you are not going to get the engagement which you are looking for.

Next thing to take care of would be making sure the influencer you are thinking about working with has a high engagement rate. If people are not tuning into his/her page, they probably won't see your ads as well. There are some tools you use to find that out, but if someone is not getting at least 5-10% of their followers' likes, meaning if they have 100k followers and they are not getting at least 5-10k likes, then the chances are the followers are not engaging.

This would also show you if the followers are BOTs or not, meaning if they have bought followers or if they are real followers.

Now, let's talk about how to get a shout from these Instagram pages. Message them directly saying that you want a shout out. Then once you guys work out a deal, ask them for a "story shout

out" as those work the best and ask for a 12-hour story shout out, all the followers will see your advertisement within the 12 hours so no need to advertise it longer than you should.

With that being said, let's now discuss the third method.

Blogs and Emails

This method works great! If someone has already bought from you once, and they liked the product or your services, odds are they will buy from you again. Using tools like creating your own blogs or anything of that nature can work beautifully for you to get sales and or to get some traffic onto your store. So, there are a lot of ways you can get free traffic. We will only be talking about the two main ones today which would be creating a blog and collecting an email list. Now, there is a downside to this method, and it could take some time to get traffic to your blog and collecting email list so don't consider this method if you want fast results.

Using blogs and email list to promote your products and services have been used for some time now. A lot of successful drop-shipping businesses solely use this method for advertising their products and services. So it works, and it works great! Just remember, it won't work right away as it takes time. Now with that said, here are the three things that you need to worry about before you start advertising with this method.

- Create a blog
- Get traffic on the blog
- Collect email subscribers
- Email them not SPAM!

The first thing you need to do is to create a blog. You will need to create a blog in order for you to actually start collecting emails. So, how you going to actually collect emails is quite simple. Once you have created a blog, I want you to begin publishing about the niche or subject with relates to your store or product. For example, if your online store or your product is about fishing, then write a blog about "how to ice fish" etc. Make sure the blog you write is filled with knowledge. People would not want to subscribe to a blog if it

35

is not exciting or providing them with great tricks and tips about the niche.

Now, once you have created a blog and written your first blog, you will now need to start promoting your blog to the right people. This can be done for free. All you have to do is go on Google and search up similar blogs posted in the 24-hour mark time. Go on their blog's comment section and tell every reader to check out your link! It works excellent and equals free traffic.

After you have started to get some traffic onto your website, it will now be time to collect some emails. In order for you to receive emails, offer them something. So, if your blog and store are related to fitness, offer them a free workout plan if they enter their email! Everyone wants free stuff, so make sure you provide it to them. This should help you collect your email list, and I have personally built up around 10,000 email lists using this technique, so make sure you use it.

Once you have a decent amount of emails, you can now start promoting your products, But there is one thing you should remember, that is not spam! People do not like to see a sales email every day so make sure you space it out. Ideally, here is how you should go about emailing your potential client. For the first four days, send them an educational email like "how to fish" or "how to work out." Again, something related to your website, and then, on the fourth day, you can try and promote your product. This strategy works typically for me, and I am sure that it would work for you.

With all the tools provided to you, you should now be able to start your very own drop-shipping store. Remember, it takes time and effort to get to where you want to. But once you do get to a point where the money is coming in, it will become very passive and will overall help you to live the life you had always wanted to.

CHAPTER 5
Blogging 101

If you are on the fence about starting a blog or you have just started one, let me tell you why you have made the right decision of starting your very own blog or if you are about to. I think advanced readers can agree that blogging is one of the most creative ways to express one's thoughts. I remember starting my blog just to help people and express my views with the help of the internet.

Fortunately for me, blogging helped me with the needs I was looking for. It helped me express my opinions just the way I wanted to, and it honestly made me more creative. My first blog was related to the "how to make money online" niche, and I remember the first month I uploaded it, I got around 180 visitors to my site. I know for some people this isn't a lot of traffic, but for a beginner merely trying to express his thoughts into words, it was an accomplishment, to say the least.

Truthfully, the main reason why I started this blog was to promote my business and get some sales. Also, I just wanted to expand my brand and spread my knowledge in the niche I was in. Well, I didn't know that you can make money out of blogs until a couple of months into it. So, as I started to connect with people online, one of the bloggers told me to add Google Adsense to my blog to earn some cash. So, I took him up on his advice. So, a couple of months in, I was already getting some traffic to my blog and once I started using paid ads on my blog, I began to make money! I remember my first payout was $100 and I was so excited. It was my first time making money online, hence, the excitement.

As the months went by, my blog began to grow and start making more money. Little did I know I would be making money from a platform which I was merely using to promote my business. So, by now, I am making more than $1,000 a month from this blog. Which I know isn't much, but hey, I am making money for free and while promoting my business.

Then, after some time, a company messaged me and asked me to promote their product on a blog post, and they will pay me $400. I thought to myself, if I keep getting these leads at least twice a month, I can easily make $2,000 a month by merely writing 3k words explaining what the product is capable off and giving my opinion on it. I can't lie; this blogging stuff is really starting to grow on me. I am making money online! That's the dream.

After a year of blogging, I discover something called affiliate marketing. For those of you who don't know what affiliate marketing is, it is merely a commission you get if someone buys a product through your link. The exact words to myself were "well I get a lot of traffic to my blog anyway so why not make some extra cash." Well, I made the right decision. Within a couple of months, I went from making $2,000 a month to almost $15,000 a month by simply becoming an affiliate marketer with the help of the traffic to my blog.

What started as a simple way to promote a business turned into something which is now making me enough money to give up my business overall. Not only did blogging provide me with a platform to express myself and also to help promote my business, but most importantly helped me make a living.

Now, for any beginner here wanting to quit blogging or not start blogging, in general, let me ask you a question, do you want to connect with people with your ideas and thoughts while making a great living? If the answer is yes, then start your blog now or after you are done reading this book. And if the answer is no, then pass on this book to someone starting a blog.

Listen, I know it's hard to make that decision of getting started but once you do, there is really no looking back here. You will soon be living the life you want to live by taking action now and not one year from now. Look at me after some years of blogging, I now entirely make a living out of my blog, and it is the best decision I have made so far.

Truth be told, you don't have to waste your time working a 9-5 in order to make money and live for the weekend. Look, I can say with no hesitation that blogging is the way to go if you want to make money fast and make a living while working. If you follow the steps in this book, you will get there quicker than I did.

Niche

Picking out a niche is probably one of the most important things you need to consider when you are first starting out your blog. The best way to decide which niche to pick for you and your blog would be to find all your interests, what do you like to do in your spare time? Is it fishing or skateboarding? Whatever you decide to write your blog on needs to be something you're truly passionate about as it will show on your writings. If you're not interested in a topic your blog is on then, you won't get a lot of traffic, as compared to your blog's topic being on something you are genuinely interested.

As by now, you can see the importance of picking out the right niche. Once you have picked out the right niche, which truly resonates with your personality and who you are, then we are ready to go! Now, once you have decided on which niche your blog will be based in, it would be the time to investigate it even further.

As a blog writer, the first thing you need to make sure of would be to find out everything you can about the niche you will be writing on, and it is imperative that you do so as it will only lead to further success with collecting your ideal prospects. Now, if you followed the first step by picking out a niche you are already passionate about, then it would be easier for you to find information about the niches' latest news, etc. But regardless, there are a couple of ways to go about finding absolutely everything about your niche which we will be covering today in this chapter.

More specifically, we will be discussing the three ways on how to find out everything about your niche in order to stay up to date with trends and new topics. The first thing you can do in order to find out more about your niche would be to use social media fan pages, as they do talk about the latest news and updates. The second method would be to read up on the top blogs in your niche, and the third one would be to learn more historical things about your niche as I will show you how it can help you.

Social media

Now, social media is one of the most powerful ways to stay connected with the latest news online. Especially for niche-based topics, I think we can all agree on the fact that the general population now relies on social media for the latest news rather than using traditional methods like newspaper or news channel. Not saying that newspapers or news channels are dead or useless, but most of the time, social media delivers the news to us faster than any news channel or newspaper would.

Well, it is a no-brainer for most of the bloggers to stay up-to-date with the news and latest trends utilizing social media as their tool. Now, there are three leading social media websites which I would recommend you use, and the first one would be Facebook. As we all are aware, Facebook is one of the biggest and most popular social media websites. If there is anything even remotely related to your niche, Facebook will have news and updates for you. The second one would be to use Instagram, and I would highly recommend using Instagram to stay up to date with any news or controversies regarding your niche.

Finally, the third social media platform I would recommend to be used would be Snapchat. Recently, Snapchat has started to use its platform to provide its users with some news and updates on the most niches you can think about. Quite frankly, the stories are subpar at the most, but sometimes, they really help you keep the mind flowing and do more research on a specific topic. With that note, let us get into the specifics on how these three platforms can be used to your advantage.

Let's first discuss Facebook. By now, Facebook has around 2.27 billion active users, so it is safe to say that Facebook has every news and up-to-date trends you can think about. More specifically, if your goal is to learn more about your niche and its latest trends, then consider joining fan pages related to your niche. Facebook has a lot of fan pages in a lot of different niches, so don't worry, and you will find a fan page related to your niche. The reason for having a fan page on Facebook is to provide the fans with its latest news and updates regarding what is happening in that niche, so definitely start using this platform to your advantage.

Instagram is a platform everyone has heard about by now. Slowly but surely, Instagram is starting to take over Facebook and become the next most prominent social media platform. The reason is simple. It is because it is so fun yet easy to use. Similar to Facebook, there are a lot of fan pages with every single niche you can think of. Use this tool to keep yourself updated with all the latest trends and topics related to your niche.

Thirdly, we will be covering the platform known as Snapchat. Some of you might know about this social media platform, but it is mainly used by many to share photos which they might have taken. Snapchat has a feature known as "the story." The main reason for having stories on the Snapchat page is relatively simple. It is to provide users with the latest news and updates, but the only drawback is that the niche section isn't as "filled up" as something like Facebook. But as I previously said, it gets the mind flowing. The niches covered on Snapchat are very broad niches, granted this is a relatively new feature, so we cannot expect it to compete with Facebook and Instagram.

Top blogs

Yes, you read it right. Using other blogs related to your niche for inspiration to get ideas and stay up to date with your blog works excellent. Quite frankly, this method sometimes works even better in comparison to using social media to stay updated with news related to your blog. So, how you utilize this method is very straightforward. The first thing you will do is to make sure the blog you are reading up on is highly respected in your niche. Secondly, you will try and see what the latest trend is in the blogging community.

For instance, if your blog is about health and fitness, then read up on all the top blogs in that niche and see what they are posting. Most of the time, they will post controversial post on the latest topics in that niche, which will not only keep you up to date with the niche but it will also give you some great ideas on how to write your blog post. Just make sure to cross-reference information in the blog post, as sometimes, bloggers can "twist up" the news. Just make sure you have the most accurate information.

Finally, using recent articles or latest updates from big news websites will work, too. Articles are very similar to a blog post, but just a little more authentic. Use the most recent articles which provide you with the latest news or discoveries in your niche to further your knowledge. Most of the time, the information provided will be accurate. That is if the website is of a big news channel. So, definitely consider using this platform.

History

Finding out the history of your niche can help you a long way when it comes to creating new topics. Now, it is essential that you stay up to date with the latest news in your niche by using the methods provided above. But if your goal is to become a true master in your niche, then it is not only important, but it is necessary that you know about every single thing there is about your niche, which of course includes the history.

Being aware of the history in your niche will help you with a lot of things when it comes to creating your content, more specifically, two things. First of all, help you understand newer information better, and secondly, help you create your own original content. So, first of all, knowing the history of your niches will help you identify the latest news better. Since most of the latest news or findings are sort of related to a prior history of the niche, let's take the health and fitness niche as an example. In the health and fitness industry, most news and research are cross-referenced with older information, since you might have heard or read of blog titles such as "Forty-year-old information was correct after all."

If you only decided to read up on the latest news and had not considered reading up on the history of the niche, then chances are you might not know anything about the information in the latest news which might have been historical before. Can you see why knowing everything including history is essential? It is because trends play itself out every time. Trust me, everything thing done in the past will be back in trend sooner than later. For instance, if you look at fashion, you will notice that the latest trend is inspired or is ultimately brought back from past trends.

I will keep saying it again and again; you need to get yourself aware and knowledgeable about the events that took place in the past related to your niche. If you want to make your blog stand out and have some great content flowing, then there is no shying away from learning the history of the blog. I know history could get boring, but if you want to grow your blog and get those potential leads, then your information needs to be of the utmost quality. People who are genuinely interested in the niche your blog is in will know the ins and outs of the niche, and to turn these beautiful people into potential customers, you basically need to become an expert in the niche you are in. If you follow the steps in this book, you will become one of the experts in no time.

My recommendation would be to read up on older blog posts and forums to find out more about the history of your niche. You can even read older books on your topic if you prefer that. Just make sure you have some time throughout the day to look up the history of your niche and absorb as much knowledge as you can.

This chapter should give you a clear idea on how to start your very own blog, more importantly, why. Blogging is one of the best ways to earn a lot of money online and to even get up to $300 a day. I hope this chapter was informative to you and we will see you in the next chapter.

CHAPTER 6
How To Make Money From Blogging

Affiliate Marketing

Believe it or not, affiliate marketing is one of the most common ways to make money from your blog. The truth is that bloggers make most of their money from affiliate marketing. It is very easy to start collecting your commission checks from your very own blog post, as we will show you how to do so. The top main affiliate programs to go with would be Amazon and Clickbank, as they will allow you to have a vast majority of the products to advertise, and also, this will allow making more money. Finding products to sell won't be so hard. It will be marketing which will be the problem. The best way to go about marketing would be to collect emails.

Email Marketing

Hope you're excited; we will be discussing how to create a vast email list from a single post. I just want to remind you of the fact that having an extensive email list doesn't mean that you will get a whole lot of sales, it is much better to have 1,000 emails which are engaging rather than having 10,000 emails which aren't as engaging. Either way, you need to make sure that you have the right amount of participating email addresses in order to start earning some money quickly.

For some people who don't know how this works, collecting emails gives you the ability to contact people. Meaning that you will reach people if you have something to sell, so if you have around 1,000 emails and you email a product to sell to the 1,000 emails, you have an affiliate or a product of your own. Let's just say that your product or affiliate product is worth around $40 in profit to you, and you only have 10% of the people from your email list buy it. You have now made $4,000 in one day. Let's say you have 10,000 engaging emails, and only 10% of your email list buys from you, you have now made $40,000 in one day!

Hopefully, by now, you're getting the idea of how powerful collecting an email list can be concerning making money rather quickly. That said, let's go through some tips and tricks on how to grow your email list rather swiftly and effectively. Before you get into tips, let's first discuss how you will be storing these emails. There are two websites or tools you can use to do so, and the first one would be to use mailchimp.com. It is free up to 1,000 emails, and then you have to pay after. If you're a beginner with no money, then this might work a little better for you, if not, then there are plenty of other apps you can use online to collect email.

Either way, you need to figure out how you will be collecting these emails for your blog. So, without further ado, let us talk about the three things we need to make sure of before we can start to make money with one singular post. Now, there are two most prominent ways to do so. First would be to use a technique where you offer something of value to the readers also known as an ethical bribe. The second method would be to merely have a pop-up show every time they visit your page. These are two simple yet effective techniques.

Ethical Bribe

We have all done it before, and we had all entered our email previously because someone was using this method correctly. Look, you can never go wrong using this method to collect emails. This is by far the easiest most effective way to receive emails without a doubt, and yes, as the title says, we are talking about using the ethical bribe to collect some profitable email. Now, how this works is when someone enters your blog or website, a pop-up will show up. What that pop-up will do is offer a gift to the people reading the blog. So, for instance, if your blog is about health and fitness, you will provide them something like a free eBook on different types of workouts you can do online. So, in order to unlock the gift, they will have to enter their email. Simple enough, you offer them something they want or like for free, and all they have to do is open their email.

I think we can all agree on the fact that we have entered our email to an ethical bribe. Now, there are two ways to go about it. First

45

would be to make sure that whatever you're offering in exchange for the email is relevant to your blog's niche. The second one would be to provide something they can't refuse. Let's talk about the fitness niche again. If your blog post is about fitness and you offer them a basic workout, then chances are a lot of people won't enter their emails since they can find basic exercises everywhere. Instead, provide them with a guide book on how to create their own workouts based on their problems and needs.

Do you see the difference? Instead of giving them a cookie cutter workout which they can find anywhere, you have managed to provide them with something they can honestly take some knowledge out of, essentially offering them something of value.

One other way to offer an ethical bribe would be to give your readers a chance to win a free product if they enter their emails. I know some people who have used this method to collect a lot of money, but mostly, this is how it works. The first thing you will do is offer readers something they can't resist. It could be money or it could be a chance to win a free iPod to one lucky winner.

What this would do is create a great buzz around the blog and more people would enter in their email to simply win money or iPod. Make it a draw, so people get excited and spread the word around. Unfortunately, you might have to invest some money upfront but it works, and it is totally worth it. Again, you don't have to use this method. It just merely works great, that's all. Don't worry; the free eBook method also works great!

Pop-ups

The second thing I would like to talk about would be to use generic pop-ups. It is quite simple and effective. Very similar to the ethical bribe, all you have to do is just ask them to enter their email, and they will be getting updates on whenever you post a new blog. This pop-up can show up anywhere on the blog website, and it doesn't have to be on the home page. It could show up on the homepage, literally anywhere until they add their email to the pop-up. Just make sure you have a great pop-up so they don't miss it and they don't second-guess adding their email.

So, to make sure your pop-up looks great, make sure you pick the right color. Using colors like plain white won't work as they don't pop so much. Use colors like red to really attract people's attention so they genuinely can't miss out. Another thing to consider would be the caption, thus again making sure that you don't input in something bland like "enter your email here." It simply sounds boring; say something like "enter your email to get updates on new amazing blogs uploading every day." This sounds better and would work better, so definitely make sure to add the right colors and the right choice of words.

Mostly, it would help if you got readers emotionally attached to the blog for them to enter their email. In order to do that, first, you need to make sure to offer them something for free which is of value to them. Again, if your blog is about fitness, you can't provide them with a cookie cutter workout plan. It needs to be of high-quality for them to enter their emails.

Secondly, you need to make sure your pop-ups look amazing, and you can't expect to get a bunch of people to enter their emails if your page looks bland. So, make sure to have bright colors on your pop-ups and also make sure have the right caption which hits them emotionally. I remember seeing this pop-up where it said something along the lines of "No thanks, I don't like free stuff" if someone decided to opt out of entering their email. That line or quote gets most people emotionally. That being said, make sure that the pop-ups have a line or quote where it gets the readers emotionally. But don't have a line like "enter your email, or you will remain fat" as it will just make you look like an insensitive person.

Hopefully, this helped you figure out how to collect emails regarding the use of these techniques in order to store emails and the ethical bribe and the pop-up techniques. Now, let us briefly touch up on how to actually make money using the email list.

How to make money?

There are two simple steps to remember in order to make money. First of all, the product or affiliate product which you will be selling has to be of the utmost quality. So, if you are selling a treadmill, for example, or if you're affiliated with a company that sells treadmill, you need to make sure that the product isn't "junk" as it will lead you to lose trust in your readers.

Now, for the most crucial step to cover. For you to actually get more people to buy from your email list and help you make heaps of money with just one post and one email, you need to make sure to email them and not spam them. Truth be told, no one likes a blogger or a marketer who makes it difficult for readers to trust them. If you keep sending them emails regarding a product or a sales pitch. Then chances are they will unsubscribe, and you need first to make sure to gain their trust and how you do that is very simple.

I like to use a technique where I email the readers informational stuff, so again if your blog is about fitness, send them one email every two days regarding new information or something helpful. Like "how to get fit in 30 days" or "ketogenic diet recipes" etc., and you need to make sure the information you provide is actually helpful to the readers. Now, here is the trick, after you have sent out at least four informational emails with no sales pitch, you can send your sales pitch on the fifth one.

So, a day before you can email your email list, ask them to check out the new blog you are about to post in 24 hours, and then once you have posted a blog, you can have the product links in that blog. Then, after 24 hours of you posting you're a blog, you can send them another email regarding the products you have to offer. Just make sure you have captured the most amounts of buyers.

This method works great, and it isn't pushy. Just make sure only to send them a sales email every four emails. Meaning the first four have to be informational and the fifth one can be a sales pitch. If you follow these two steps, you will not only grow an engaging email list, but you will also get the most sales. In order to make this even more profitable, slowly "hype up" your email list a couple of days before saying things like "make sure to check out the post in 4 days as it will blow your mind". This will further enhance you're sales and make you a lot of money. Again, get the readers as excited as you can in order to make some serious money on that one post.

With that note, I would like to conclude this fantastic yet informative chapter. Remember, that in order to make money with your email list, you need to make sure you have a place to store your email. You can use mailchimp.com or any other server; it is entirely up to you. Second, you need to make sure that you offer them an ethical bribe, and also to make sure that the bride is of high quality. It cannot be anything of a cookie cutter.

The third thing to make sure is to have a fantastic choice of color on your pop-up. Anything red works. Also, make sure you're caption hits them emotionally. Once you have managed to do that now, it would be the time to email them. Make sure your first four emails are of high-quality emails, so they become more engaged. Finally, it would be best if you made sure that the fourth email is about a product you want to sell or are affiliated with. Also, remember the fact that the product is of high quality. Remember to excite them up for your blog post a little bit in every email as it will lead them to read it more likely, and after another 24 hours, send them another email regarding the product you want to sell.

Trust me, and these techniques work like a charm. If your goal is to get the most out of your email list, you most definitely need to follow these methods listed above. With that being said, see you on the next page

CHAPTER 7
Become A Pro-Blogger

In the previous chapter, we briefly discussed the benefits of having an email list. We went into details on everything from how to build an email list to all the way on how to utilize the email list correctly in order to make the most money out of it. Now, needless to say, in order to collect email and make money, you need traffic. Currently, there is no better way to gain traffic than to make sure you're content is golden. You can't expect to gain notoriety without having great content.

So what does creating great content mean? Well, there are two ways to produce great content. The first and the most obvious way would be to make sure you're content adds value to the readers. You can't expect to make money or get traffic with a blog if you can't make the readers feel like it's worth their time. So, making sure you have value in your content is the key. The second way to attract more traffic to your blog would be to add some controversy.

Now, truth be told, everyone loves to read up on the controversy. Even if it doesn't provide them with any benefits, people will still read up on it. If you have a fashion blog, people would much rather read up on the latest gossip regarding the most trending superstar than to learn about the latest trends going on in fashion. Do you see my point? If you want to create a blog post which helps you get a whole lot of traffic, then it is best to write about the latest controversies in your niche.

There are some flaws to this technique though. Even though creating a controversial blog can help you gain a lot of attention, you need to make sure that it is done tastefully or you're brand name can be jeopardized. We will further discuss the reasons why it needs to be written or portrayed tastefully, but just remember that using this method could affect your brand image so be aware of that.

Controversy

Now, there are two types of controversies. The first one being a the debate controversy and the second one being the shocking or taboo controversy. For example, having a campaign which is belittling racists would be considered a debate controversy. Most people could agree with the fact that racism is not the best thing to partake on. Except for racist people, everyone else would find your post humorous and shareable to their friends. This would be considered a safe controversy.

Another yet so famous controversy was created by United Colors of Benetton, which made them famous. They posted a photo of a nun kissing. The idea behind it was to "unite" and have more multicultural acceptance. This would be considered a shocking or taboo controversy, and if not portrayed correctly, it could bring your brand crashing down. It's recommended to have a positive message if you want to use this type of controversy safely.

With any controversy posts, the point is this. You need to make sure whatever type of post you put up on your blog needs to have a "debatable" level to it in order to get noticed by people. But remember being debatable isn't enough. You need to make sure to correlate it with your brand to grow and get traffic.

If you need some ideas on how to make your blog post or banner more creative, there are plenty of amazing designs you can choose from in order to come up with a plan which will help you have a better understanding of which one to pick for the blog post.

So, now you have an idea on how to get traffic with posting some highly controversial post, remember to do it tastefully. My recommendation would be to, first and foremost, make it controversial, and secondly, make it so that it has a positive message, and it is imperative to do so as it will most likely not come along with negative stigma. One more thing to remember: if you really want to boom, your post should have a super controversial photo like United Colors of Benetton had.

Snowball effect

By now, you should be ready to create your controversial post. But you're not done yet, as you know, by far, the best way to get publicity to your blog would be through the use of the superpower which is social media. Social media has been used by so many people to boost their blog post to a whole nother level, so now; it's time for you to do the same.

Your controversial post will gain popularity with the help of social media and the snowball effect. Now, if you don't know what snowball effect is, then let me explain. The snowball effect is where you're blog post starts to become famous on social media and gets shared and promoted for free by users on social media. For some people, the snowball effect is a breakthrough for their blog post which will get a whole lot of traffic.

Let us not forget, most people online only use the internet for social media. Social media is the new way to get notoriety. So, if you can manage to get the snowball effect rolling and which you will with the help of social media and your controversial post, then your blog will get the traffic you want and need!

Now, there are three ways to create a snowball effect onto you're a blog post, but before we start this process, you need to make sure that you have you're blog posted and ready to go. Once your blog is posted and ready to go, you can now start to create a snowball effect. Our goal with this blog post is to make sure that it is indeed "debatable" and controversial. If it is controversial and debatable, then you don't need a lot of traffic from your end, as it will create some dangerous traffic with the help of social media and other people reposting your link on their page.

So, there are three things you need to do to get the snowball rolling. The first one would be to create backlinks. It is super-easy to do so, and I will show you how. The second thing you need to take care of would be to email all the email contacts you have on your latest upload. Finally, you need to make an effort to post your blog link on to every Facebook page there is related to your niche.

Let's talk about the first method which is to create some backlinks. Now, you should be building backlinks for your blogging regardless, but make sure to create as many backlinks as you can in the first three days of posting your blog. So, how you can create backlinks is relatively simple. What you do is go onto more famous blogs or even you're competitor's blogs and merely post a link to your blog. Now, unfortunately, most of the comments get deleted, so in order to avoid that, you need to make sure to post your link correctly.

In order to post your blog link correctly, you need to make sure you sound like a reader rather than a promoter. Instead of writing a comment saying, "Hey, check out my blog" you need to say "Check out this blog! Where they talk about blah blah what do you guys think?" Do you see the difference? You need to make sure that you sound like a reader instead of a blogger trying to create backlinks. This will work and only work if you make sure to look interested. Also as a reader, another thing to remember is that if your blog is going to have that controversial post, then you will get people promoting your blogs online and the backlinks you would have created would work wonders.

So, make sure to write comments on every blog you can find related to your niche and make sure to write predominantly on post or blogs which are trending and have been uploaded at least a week before the day you decide to comment on them. Since the blog will be new, it will get a lot of traffic and so will you with the backlinks created.

The second method would be to use your email list. Obviously, make sure you keep emailing your list a couple of days before you post your controversial blog online. This will help you get your readers excited and ready to read your blog on the day it is published. So, make sure you keep your email list updated, and once the blog is live, make sure to email them right away and see your blog post blow up.

Now, the third and final method, which is also very important, would be to post your blog links onto Facebook pages related to your niche. This works like a charm concerning getting traffic to your post and creating that snowball effect. So you need to make sure that in order to get some considerable traffic to your blog, you will have to post it on social media pages related to your niche.

Now, similar to creating backlinks on other blogs, posting on Facebook pages is the same. You can't get away with merely posting your blog onto the Facebook page as it requires your post to be approved by the admin of the page. So, in order to get your post approved, you have to do similar things as you did before, which would be to act like a follower/reader rather than just a promoter. Saying things like "check out this blog where they talk about blah blah" would work a lot better.

Make sure to post on social media platforms carefully, and make sure to only post it on to pages which are related to your niche. As posting it on random niche pages will merely make you look like a promoter, even if you post like a reader. Again, make sure you do use this social media platform as it works wonders and will get you're snowballing effect rolling faster.

In conclusion, remember that in order to get a whole lot of traffic and make money out of your post, you need to do a couple of things. First of all, it would be to create a controversial post as it will yield you the most results concerning gaining traffic. Again, make sure that the post is done tastefully as it can bring your brand name crashing if not done so, another thing to pick before you create your blog post would be to consider the two options you have, first one being debate controversy and the second one would be taboo or shocking controversy. Ideally, I would go with debate controversy as it is safer.

Secondly, you need to make sure that the post has been promoted correctly, and for you to do that, you need to take care of three things. The first one is creating backlinks on blogs. This works great if done right and will produce the snowball effect right away. The second one would be to email your list. This also works great, and most definitely needs to be exercised, and finally, let us not forget the power of Facebook pages. Make sure to promote your blog link just like the way this book has taught you to do so. After all that has been said and done, you should start to see the snowball effect in action right in front of your eyes. Just remember that it may or may not work for you the first time but keep trying. Eventually, it will. These methods listed in this chapter are the fastest ways to get traffic, so keep pushing and keep going at it; you will get your fame soon.

The PAS method

Hopefully, by now, you should have gotten something great concerning how to write a blog the right way and how to market it. Now, it is time to touch upon copywriting, and truth be told, copywriting isn't something which can be created by writing some things here and there, hoping to have some power magically. You can't expect to follow a formula and expect to have this beautiful copyright to follow. What these copyright formulas give you is a starting point or a framework which you can make as your own.

So, today, we will be talking about one of the most famous and useful copyright formulae. It has been used for some time now and still works great. Of course, we are talking about P.A.S: Problem-Agitate-Solve. It's an all-time favorite for most people as it works on everything for all kinds of marketing, landing pages, and flyers. Hopefully, by the description, you could have guessed what Problem-Agitate-Solve is all about. So without further ado, let us get into the topic and truly dissect this method.

Problem

Now, when we are talking about problems, you need to make sure that you get into the emotions of the readers and make them feel like they need to make the change to fix the problem. You need to make sure that you remind them of the problem and make them feel the pain as they are reading through the post. For example, if you're post is about a fitness tool like a foam roller, you would write, "Tired of using traditional foam rollers were getting the right spot is not only hard but impossible?"

Now, do you see what I am trying to say? You need to make sure that you bring up the problem which makes them feel like they definitely need a change. You will merely attach the problem and make them feel emotionally connected to what you wrote, plain and simple.

Agitate

Moving on to part two of the method, since you have now managed to get the readers agitated and ready to go in terms of getting them emotionally involved, it would be no time to attack the problem even further and get the readers more emotionally attached to the post. Now, one thing to make sure, you cannot wallow too much as it will fend off a lot of people. Just add some salt to the wound, while still making them feel like they have a way out.

An example would be "While you use the foam roller, it just seems like it is not helping you get to your problem areas, which can get annoying, and quite frankly, make you want to give up on foam rolling overall, but there is a way to fix this." Did you see what I did there? I really "added some salt" to the wound, and made the readers feel like they most definitely need the thing or product I am about to offer them.

Solve

Now finally, we will be discussing the final phase which would be to solve the problem. Since you have managed to get the readers more engaged and aware of their issues, it would be now time to fix the problem. This is very simple, but it has to be done the right way, you cannot sound like a salesman. Look, you need to be subtle with your closing meaning that you can't be too aggressive. If you end up being too aggressive, then the Problem and Agitate will go to waste.

Now, to make sure you don't sound too aggressive or rather like a salesperson, you need to make sure that you're more of a friend by helping them fix their problems rather than closing a sale. Here is an example, "No worries, with the help of this new foam roller, you can hit those hard to get areas! Try it out". As you can see, I was talking to my readers like I would be talking to a friend, simple and not too pushy. That is what you should be aiming for.

Example PAS

We have all been there, trying to wake up early every day so we can get more stuff done and get closer to our goals. But somehow, we end up waking about 4 hours after when we're supposed to.

Truth be told, these regular alarm clocks don't work anymore. Every day, you get one step away from achieving your goal. These snooze buttons are just not the way to go and are indeed holding you back.

But there is a way out, and luckily with the new alarm pillow on the market, it will vibrate your head until you wake up. I know I don't need old technology anymore! I'm going with snooze pillow. Get it today at snoozepillow.com.

Do you see how great this PAS is? It is really attacking people's problems and is genuinely here to fix the issue in no time. The best part is that you don't sound like a salesman. Just a friend who is helping another friend to fix the problems he or she may be facing. Hopefully, you get the idea by now.

People, just remember two things. Readers don't want to be sold to and also don't like it when they are sold to, and the readers love it when you bring out the problem and help them find a solution.

With that note, I would now like to conclude this chapter. Remember, using PAS is one of the best ways to get sales and recognition to your blog post. So, I would highly recommend that you use this method to get the most out of your post. Remember to not sound like a salesperson, instead, make sure you sound more like a person who truly wants to help your readers solve the problem which they might be facing. So make sure you bring up the problem, agitate it further, and offer your readers with a solution and the rest will be history.

CHAPTER 8
Instagram 101

In this chapter, we will be talking about Instagram and YouTube, and how you can make money out of it. The reason why the chapter only has Instagram at the top is that it is the most used platform out there. But if you combine all three platforms together, you can make some serious money. Most of the users make money from affiliate marketing, but in later chapters, we will show you how you can make even more money dabbling with different methods out there to earn more money. But for now, we will show you how to make money from this method and how to combine it with three other methods which will allow you to earn even more. Let's talk about affiliate marketing if you have no idea of how it works.

Affiliate Marketing

The best way to describe affiliate marketing would be to use an analogy. Let us say you are the president of your university and every single student in that university listens to your voice. Since you are the president of this university, a majority of the people in that university follows your advice and recommendations. When suddenly, a professor of the university offers you sell his textbook, and in return, you get a commission or a percentage of the textbook sale by promoting the professor's textbook to your audience or following.

So, in essence, this would be an example of affiliate marketing. Just what you have to do in order to get sales would be to first create a big following and then promote a product to that audience. Simple enough, right? Well, there are some tricks involved in this method in order to become successful in affiliate marketing which we will be discussing in this chapter. Now, there are a lot of ways you can start to market a product to make a commission; we will be considering how to do so by using the best methods for you to start affiliate marketing.

Now, the methods which will help you to start making money with affiliate market will be YouTube, blogging, and Instagram/Facebook page. Now, these three are the best ways to get started with your affiliate marketing business. There are some pros and cons to each of these tools; you might have to try out all three methods before you can see which one works for you and which one doesn't. Now, without further ado, let's begin with YouTube.

YouTube

YouTube was founded on February 14th, 2005, created by three former PayPal employees Chad Hurley, Steve Chen, and Jawed Karim. YouTube, at first, was created by the founders to share videos easily without facing any problems while doing so. Fast forward to November 2006, YouTube was sold to Google for USD 1.65 million. Ever since then, YouTube has not stopped growing. According to some sources, there is at least 1 billion hours' worth of videos that are being watched every day on YouTube. That goes to show how big YouTube is. Now, you might be wondering since this website is so popular, you could easily start promoting affiliate products and earn some great commissions.

Well, there are some tricks involved to do so, although there are a lot of videos watched on YouTube. On any given time of day, there are still some things you need to make sure. One is to check from your end before you can really start to promote your product on this website. Don't worry it isn't hard, just like any business; it will take some time and effort to get started.

The first thing you will need to do is to create a niche. Really think about what you are interested in. For example, if you are interested in fitness, then make a fitness channel. If you are interested in science, create a Science channel. The main thing you need to consider before you start your very own YouTube channel is to make sure that whatever your channel is about, it needs to be something you are genuinely interested in. This is the reason why people can see through everything these days. If you hate fitness and you decide to make a fitness channel, they can tell that you don't like fitness-related stuff, and therefore, don't subscribe to

59

your channel. Making sure you have love and passion for the circuit you will be building on YouTube is imperative.

The second thing we need to worry about is growing your channel or following, and if you don't have an audience on your YouTube channel, then chances are your affiliate marketing endeavors might go to fail. So, you first need to grow your YouTube channel before you can start selling affiliate products. With that being said, let us discuss how you can build your YouTube channel fast and efficiently.

Now, there are a lot of ways to do so, but the best way I would recommend is to come up with unique content. I know it sounds very cliché, but it works! Think about it. Why would someone want to follow you if you don't have something different to offer them? So, there are a lot of ways to be compatible with your content, but the first technique to make different material is to think outside the box and into the future like what would be the "new thing." Once you have figured it out, make sure you are the first one to start the trend.

Another way to start getting some more views and followers would be to have an exciting caption and clickbait. Let me give you an example of a clickbait. Recently, big YouTubers would do things like "My yearly income" and a photo of them with money as the clickbait on the video. Since everyone is curious about how much these big YouTubers make, these YouTubers directly elude people into their video and start to rank up the views, but they never reveal their income. As I said, it is merely clickbait. Now, this technique does work, but you can't use it every time, as it will lead to some drops in your followers, etc. so, use it with caution.

.

Finally, the last technique I would recommend would be to collaborate with YouTubers who already have a big following. Before you work with one of the big YouTube channels, make sure their channel is related to your channel. Collaborating with a more significant channel won't be easy or free. I would say 1 out of 10 will agree upon doing a "collab video" with you and finally work out a deal either by an upfront payment or a shared partnership of the video. There is some money involved, but it is totally worth it as this technique works the best in order to grow your YouTube channel and business.

Now, after you have managed to grow your YouTube channel to a substantial level—ideally, a 100k followers or subscribers—it would take no time to promote products from which you can earn an affiliate commission. Again, remember to promote a product which is related specifically to your YouTube channel. Don't expect to sell a PlayStation 4 on a channel connected to fitness. It is not that people won't buy—they probably won't—but it makes you look like a salesman, which is not the look that you should be going for. So, if you want to earn some affiliate commission, make sure the product is related to your channel and niche.

There are many websites you can use to start earning an affiliate commission, but the two leading sites I would recommend is ClickBank and Amazon. Let us cover ClickBank first. ClickBank is an online video course website that sells courses from a health-related niche to a making-money-online niche, so as you can see, it has a broad spectrum of courses available on its site. You can earn up to 75% of the commissions on each sale, and it is straightforward to do so if you have a following. All you have to do is review the video course and give your audience an honest review of the product. Make sure you add your affiliate link in the description below of the YouTube channel in order to earn commissions.

The second one is Amazon. As we know, Amazon is the biggest e-commerce website in the world right now. On top of that, they sell anything you can imagine, so it doesn't matter what niche you are in. You can find a related product to your niche. That said, there are some pros and cons to this website. The disadvantages are that the commission rates are lower compared to ClickBank. There is no exact percentage of commission you will get, but 75% of commission on Amazon is super hard to find as compared to ClickBank. Now, the positive is that once someone even clicks your affiliate link, you will be getting a commission on everything they buy for the next 48 hours. This is where the lower commission rate makes up for Amazon. Again, if you decide to use Amazon as your source of the affiliate partner, make sure you try out the product and give a proper review.

Instagram/Facebook Page

This is also a fantastic technique to start earning those affiliate commissions. So how this works is quite similar to YouTube. You will first need to attract a following to your page, and then you can start to promote your products slowly. Now, to explain this process instead is this: no audience = no sales. Therefore, our primary goal is to start getting our Instagram page bigger, which would equate to more affiliate commission.

The first method would be setting up a Facebook page which would be specific to your niche. Now, after you have created an Instagram account and a Facebook page, start promoting both pages only by purchasing shoutouts from bigger pages related to your niche. After that is done, you will slowly begin to grow your Instagram/Facebook page, but one thing to remember is that you don't want to stop posting content on your Instagram/Facebook page as it will result to a drop of followers and engagement rate.

The second method to grow your Instagram page is to use a technique known as "follow-unfollow." It is pretty self-explanatory. What you have to do is follow users hoping that they would follow you back and then eventually unfollow them. This technique works if your goal is to gain some following quickly. That said, this is not the best way for long-term growth so keep that in mind. Start following people and unfollow them after three days or so.

Finally, let us talk about how to make money with affiliate marketing on Instagram. So, after you have a following off around 100k, you will then start to notice people will pay you money to have their product on your page. You can also do affiliate marketing with ClickBank, but it just works better when you promote on Instagram using the "shoutout" technique.

Using all three at once

Now, ideally, this is how it should be. Using YouTube, Blogging, and Instagram all at once will yield you the best results. So, if you really want to make some serious cash with affiliate marketing, here is how you do it. You will first create a brand. For example, if you're into fitness, you will create a YouTube channel, blog, and

Instagram/Facebook account with a brand name that you came up with. Now, you will merely use all the techniques listed in this chapter to make sure all three sales channels—YouTube, blog, and Instagram—grow and flourish.

How much money can you make?

Now, this is a question that can't be answered straight away. You see, if your goal is to put in minimal time and make it as passive as possible, you can realistically make anywhere from $100 to $1,000 a month. But if you really want to make some serious cash and if you utilize all three sales channels while using the techniques above, you can make $100,000 to $1,000,000 a month. I have personally seen some pay stubs of the top affiliate marketers, and they surely make more than a million dollars a year, so if you are willing to put in the hard work, you can seriously make some fantastic cash.

All that said I would now like to conclude this chapter by saying this: With affiliate marketing, the choice is yours. You can choose to make an extra $1,000 a month by doing some work here and there, or you can honestly take your income to the next level! Again, the choice is yours.

CHAPTER 9
How To Make Money From Instagram Page

If you remember previously, we talked about how to make money from Instagram and YouTube. In this chapter, we will show you all the opportunities out there, which will allow you to make tons of money. Affiliate marketing is a great way to make money; however, making your own Instagram page to grow and to make money out of the niche people who follow you can be one of the best ways to make money. One of the ways to do that is to make cool merchandise based on your Instagram or Facebook page, allowing you to make the most money.

Now, you might have heard of this topic before, but if not, let me explain to you how this works. Selling merchandise is merely selling a t-shirt with a distinctive logo to a client. It could be anything like shoes, pillowcases, etc. But most of the time, this is used for selling t-shirts. How this works is simple. Specific websites or apps allow you to add any logo your heart desires and sell it to customers. It is similar to drop-shipping, since you don't have to see the products, and it ships out directly to your customers.

This method is probably the most trending right now regarding making money online since it is so new, you can make money with it rather quickly. Now, there are a couple of things we need to take care of before you can go ahead and start your very own business of selling merchandise. Now, there are a lot of platforms you can use to start you're very personal shop such as Amazon Merch, Redbubble, Tasty, and your very own Shopify. It is entirely up to you which website you use to get started with, and luckily, the start-up cost for all is very cheap and reasonably affordable, so you don't need to worry about investing a lot of money into it. All you need to worry about is the monthly payment of websites and the cost to get a logo design done, that's all.

With that said, here are three things you need to take care of before you can start your business of selling merchandise. 1. Find a niche 2. Make an Instagram/Facebook page 3. Advertising. So, all these things are essential if you want to be successful in this business. So, without further ado, let us get into it.

Finding a niche

Finding a niche is very important for you to actually to make this business profitable. Think about it? Why would someone want to buy your t-shirt? It is merely a t-shirt. Whereas, if you make a meme t-shirt, everyone who is a fan of memes would be interested in buying your product. It is essential that you find a niche you would want to sell into.

Now, there are a lot of niches to get into. Your job is to find one where you can sell t-shirts relating to the niche. Now, there are a lot of examples of this. But I will use one for the readers so they can get a better idea. So, if you ever stumble upon fitness gurus or fitness channels on YouTube, these guys solely use these methods to make and distribute it to the buyers, since they have a large following of people who want to buy from them.

The beauty of finding a niche in this business model is that you can make any topic or niche profitable business. So, if you like bowling, you can create cool bowling logos and sell it to people who would be interested in bowling. As long as you have a cool logo, you can sell your t-shirts. Also, you need to get traffic on you're the page, but we will get into that topic later on in this chapter.

Listen, you don't need to find a specific niche. You can enter any niche your heart desires and sell it on there as long as the logo looks cool and you have people in that niche become aware of your t-shirt or any merchandise for that matter.

YouTube

Now, making a YouTube account is very easy. If you have a Gmail account, then chances are you already have a YouTube account for you to upload on. Once you have the YouTube account, pick a niche and start to advertise your page on there. YouTube is one of the hottest social media out there, in regards to building an audience. Essentially, your goal is to build up audiences all around your niche's specific page like YouTube, blog, Instagram page, so you have more places to reach a potential audience.

Growing a YouTube audience is a bit complicated, which is why we recommend you start by building both Instagram and YouTube pages simultaneously. That way, you can get your viewers to grow faster and to get more benefits out of it. Another way you can actually make money from YouTube would be to start monetizing your videos. Once you reach 1,000 subscribers, you will have the ability to monetize your videos. Hence, allowing you to make money from it. Then, once you have achieved 1,000 subscribers, you can then start to sell your merchandise. This way, you will be making money from YouTube, and you will start to get sales for your merchandise. As always, you can even begin to promote products to earn an affiliate commission.

That way, you can make money from three different avenues from one source. Remember, it is always good to have as many streams of income as possible in this day and age. Really try and capitalize on as many income avenues as possible. That way, you can start to earn more money sooner and you will have better chances of scaling up even higher. This goes for any income stream listed in this book. Hopefully, that helps you to make more money.

Make Instagram/Facebook page

Now, once you have found out which niche you will be getting into, it would soon be time to make an Instagram and a Facebook page on that subject. Now, most people don't talk about this, but making a niche specific page and growing it to a big following can get you a bunch of sales. As this would be targeted advertising, you will first gain people's trust by posting amazing photos and logos on your page, so people follow. And once it grows out to be a more prominent page, you can then start selling merchandise to them, and it will sell.

There are a couple of ways to grow your Instagram page. One of them would be to buy followers online. However, that isn't effective if you want to improve your brand and get more sales. Remember, it is much better to have 1,000 followers that are active than 10,000 followers that are inactive. Our goal is to make an Instagram page which will help you make money, not boost your ego. Now, to organically grow your Instagram page, here are the top 5 things to do: 1. Be active on your account 2.Follow and unfollow 3. Post high-quality photos 4. Get paid promotions from bigger pages 5. Join an engagement group.

So, the first thing we will be covering would be being active on Instagram, being active on Instagram means that you are continually liking and commenting on photos and videos on Instagram. What this does is to get your account out there and be visible to the people who might be interested in following you. Once you start liking and commenting on the photos and videos on a more prominent Instagram page, often you will begin to notice your channel is getting free publicity and people will start to follow you. So, make sure you are doing this religiously every day to grow your Instagram page.

The second thing would be to use a method known as "follow-unfollow." Essentially, what your goal with this method is to follow as many active users as possible, and then unfollow after three days or so. There are some online tools which will take care of this process for you, so you can either go that route, or you can go the other direction and do this manually. If you do go manually, make sure to write down their names, so you can unfollow them after three days or so. This technique still works to gain quick followers in a hurry. Make sure that you are utilizing it, especially in the beginning.

The third method would be to make sure you provide users with some high-quality photos, and this is crucial for your Instagram to grow. If your page is about camping and outdoor activities, and you post landscape photos, they can't be of and quality. You need to make sure you have high-quality images, and you can use other Instagram pages photos which are of high quality but always make sure to tag them on your post. One company who has done this successfully is outdoor_hack. They are a Shopify-based account, and even though they don't have any photos taken especially for them, they still have managed to grow and make money. So, if you are looking for some inspiration, I would check that page out on Instagram.

The fourth thing you can do would be to use bigger pages online to promote your page. How this works is that you pay them money for a 24 hour or 12-hour shout out. Most of the time, they post it on their story or feed. This works great if you have some money to invest, merely getting shout-outs from bigger pages can help you grow your page quite rapidly.

Now, finally, we will talk about engagement groups. This is the method most people use to take their page/pages to the next level. This method will make your page skyrocket in followers, and of course, more sales for your merchandise business. An engagement group is a group of pages similar in size. What everyone in this group will do is whenever you post a photo, they will like and comment on it the picture, and you will also have to love others photos and comment on them.

Every engagement group has different rules, but most of them pre-decide when everyone is going to post online. Everyone in the group has to like and comment on that specific post within the allotted time period of typically 30 minutes, and if you don't follow the rules, you will be kicked out of the group, period. So make sure to follow the rules, and finally, make sure to follow all the four steps above so you can actually utilize this tool correctly and get the most out of it.

Now, most of my readers might be wondering, why did I ramble on growing a niche based Instagram account? Here is the reason why most people won't tell you this, but this business model won't work correctly if you don't have a niche based Instagram/Facebook page. So, if you want to make money out of this business model, having a niche page with a big following is a big part of your success. Now, this takes time. If you want to get quick sales fast, you will have to advertise your product.

Advertising

Now, once you have created a Facebook page, you can use that page to utilize Facebook's advertising services to promote your products. It is the exact same process as the one described in chapter 6 so make sure to check that out. However, we again come back to Instagram advertising to make money. It just works so much better than any other method.

Instagram, as I said before, is a great place to advertise your products, especially for the merchandise business since it is such a niche based one. So, if your goal is to get quick sales on your page, you can use this method. When we advise on Instagram most of the time, you will use a technique called "Instagram influencer."

Similar to promoting your page for more followers you will find an Instagram page which is related to your topic which also has a big following, then you will get a paid shoutout from them and see the sales come in. People who are in the business of selling merchandise online can say this is one of the fastest ways of getting sales. There are three things you need to take care of before you start advertising on an Instagram page.

- Finding the right influencer
- Making sure they don't have any BOTs
- How much engagement are they getting

As you know by now, in order to get sales and make money, you need to make sure you are promoting your product to the right audience. So you cannot promote a fitness shirt on a page that is about global warming, Make sure the page you decide to encourage on is about what you are trying to promote.

Just a little side note, make sure whichever page you choose has over 300k followers. Now, this depends from niche to niche, but this a good rule of thumb to follow when picking out your influencer.

Now, finding an account in your niche with over 300k followers is tremendous but what's their engagement like? The truth is some pages have "BOTs," meaning they have bought followers for their page. There are a couple of ways to find out if that's the case or not, but if someone is not getting at least 5-10% of their followers like their post, meaning if they have 100k followers and they are not getting at least 5-10k likes, then the chances are their follows have been bought.

So, in order to get a shout from these Instagram pages, you will have to message them directly saying something along the lines of wanting a shoutout. Once you have decided on a price, you can start to promote your product on their page once they receive the payment. One thing to remember is that there is no need to get a 24-hour shout out for a product ad. All of the followers on the page will see your advertisement within the 12 hours, so no need to advertise it longer than you should.

How much money can you make?

Now, this totally depends on you, but you can make as much as $1,000 to as much as you want. The sky is indeed the limit. This is the same as Shopify. You can make a lot of money with this method, make sure you have a niche brand and also make sure to grow it as big as you can. You can become a millionaire, if not a billionaire, with this method. But if you want to make some extra cash on the side, it would be very easy to do so with this method.

So, remember to follow everything that is said in this chapter if you want to start earning some cash. The biggest secret revealed is to grow your very own Instagram pages. This is something that isn't talked about so much. Creating logos and other aspects of the business is very easy to do but if you want to grow your business and take it to the next level, make sure to create and improve your Instagram account as quickly as possible. Also, make sure to pick a niche in which you have interest and passion for it will more likely grow bigger for you as compared to others.

CHAPTER 10
Future Of Passive Income

If you thought that we were going to tell you something like "new way to make money online," then you are entirely wrong. When people think of passive income, they think about sitting at home collecting money. All the methods we talked about so far in this book where passive, but the two main ways we are going to talk about in this chapter as the most passive methods out there. These methods will ensure passive income. That means you will make money while sitting at home. These two streams of income have been used in the past, and I believe the future of passive income.

Stock Market

A stock market is also a form of trading. It has been used by big investors like Warren Buffet to make some serious cash. The stock market was founded on March 8th, 1817 in New York City U.S.A. The stock market was created for people to start investing in companies for the company to get more funds for growth. Eventually, as the companies would grow, the stock prices would go up for the specific company. So, for the people who had some money invested in the company, they would sell those stocks for a profit which would mean more money in their pockets. So, in a nutshell, that is how stock market trading was invented.

Now, this method has some pros and cons to it so let us go through them. To start with the advantages, the first positive is, of course, you can make money using this process. The second positive would be it is entirely passive compared to other methods in this book. All you have to do is check up the stock market frequently, and you should be good. Just like anything in this world, there are some cons. The first significant con would be that you can lose you invested money. It is imperative that you do your research on the company before you decide to invest in that company.

The second con would be irregular, what I mean by that is this. Let us say you buy a stock at $1.30 a piece and a couple of days go by and the stock is now $2.00. Most of the people would rather wait, but sometimes, the stock would come plummeting down to $0.80 a piece which would make you lose money. Or if you decide to sell it at $2.00 per share, you would still make good money, but if the next day it shot up to $3.00 per share, you would be regretting your decision.

Look, what I am trying to say is this. Utilizing the stock market to make money is like a rollercoaster ride. You will have your ups and downs, and you will face some significant losses sometimes or some significant gains. Although there are ways to avoid the considerable injuries with the methods I will provide, the main thing to remember is not to get greedy as it might make money sometimes, but you can come crashing down.

There are two methods to make money utilizing the stock market which we will be going through today. The first one is "Growth stocks" and the second one would be "Mutual funds."

Growth Stocks

Growth stocks, also known as "buy low sell high" is one of the most common techniques used by many investors. Although this method takes time and effort, it can yield you with some good returns. Now, the principle behind this method is this, find a company with cost per stock that is low, and then once it goes up, sell it and enjoy the profits you made. Simple enough, right? Well, there are some things to be learned before you go about doing so, specifically three things.

- Research about the company
- Patients and discipline
- Continued research

To begin with, let's talk about how to research the company you will be investing in. As we know, there are a lot of companies in this day and age. Picking out the right company to spend it can be somewhat tricky. So, this is where the extensive research comes in before you pay in one. To be clear, there is no right or wrong company to be investing in. There are a lot of companies which will go up, and you have to pick the one you believe in. To find out if the stocks of a particular company will go up or not, it requires a couple of steps. The first thing you need to do is to check out last year's report on the company and their stock prices.

Check to see if the stock prices have steadily been going up or not and are it still continuing on. The second method would be to make sure that the company is up is to do something big which will help the company grow, for example. Canada made marijuana legal which equated to all the marijuana dispensaries stock prices to go up in Canada. So, what I mean by doing research is to see if anything significant is happening to the company or the market the company is in.

Being patient and having a certain amount of discipline is imperative for your growth and success in this market in order for you to make money and not to lose money while investing in stocks. Truth be told, you can make some severe cash overnight with this method or make some fantastic returns a couple of years down the road. Don't get impatient and sell your stocks when you have an idea of the company and if it is going to be making significant moves soon.

On the other hand, don't get greedy. If the stocks are coming up fast, then they will come down just as soon in most cases. Don't get greedy wanting for more money. Sell it once you have made some good money out of those stocks. This would be where your discipline comes into factor. Finally, I would like you to remember that investing in stocks requires some "gut feeling." Not everything is going to be calculated in stock market spending. After you have done your research and decided to buy stocks, you might have to go by gut feelings sometimes to sell your shares.

Finally, what you will have to take care of is continued research on the company. Now, making sure to stay up to date with the company's news in which you invested in is imperative for your growth and success. This will give you an idea of when to sell and when not to sell your stock. For instance, let us say you find out the company you invested in might notice a drop in its stock price. Merely make sure to sell it before you lose money or vice versa.

Continued research and updates will give you an idea of when to sell and when not to sell.

Mutual funds

This method is a little bit easier to get started with as it comes with a lower risk. Mutual funds are when your money is managed by professionals and is invested in different companies by them. Although there is a cut taken by the professionals, in the end, it is still a safer and effective way if you want to make money as compared to "Growth Stock." Since you won't have to worry about doing research online and checking out every little detail about the company, it will be more of a "passive investment" which will make you money later on.

So, if you want to make money without spending too much time doing research and other things which are related to "growth stocks" as it is less of a risk, go ahead, but you won't make as much money as you could be making with "growth stocks."

How much money can you make?

Now, this would depend entirely on the market and how much you put in. The stocks game is "the more you put in, the more money you will make," so if you want to make more, you will have to invest more. There is no estimate on how much you can potentially make, and you can make $1,000 profit up to a $1,000,000 profit. It depends on luck and how much you invest in the company. Like I said previously, if you want to play it safe, I would recommend you invest in some mutual funds, even though the returns won't be as good as "growth stocks," it will still yield you some good money without the risk.

Remember that investing in the stock market is a gamble. You might make some money or lose some money. If you do what is advised in this book, chances are you will make money. Many full-time day traders make money solely off the stock market. But you need to remember that the market is unpredictable and anything could happen anytime, so if I were you, I would invest some money on the side rather than to make this a full-time job as it is not so secure.

Once you do spend, don't forget to do your research and to make sure that you don't pay more than what you can afford. Again, if "growth stocks" scare you, then invest in some mutual funds. Sometimes, it is good to take some risks as you don't know where it will take you. Remember to be safe and smart with your money and don't get too greedy as it could lead you to lose your hard-earned money which is the last thing we want to do.

Options Trading

Just like the previous method, this method will also be a bit "theoretical," so please read it a couple of times if you don't understand it fully the first time. Now, there are two types of options trading. One is the call options and the other is the put options. So, in this chapter, we will be going through the two options. We will discuss how they work. So, without further ado, let us get into it.

Call options

To explain the call options, we will be using an analogy. Let's say you work in the automotive industry. You know the ins and outs of it. You also know exactly how much a specific car is worth and if it will go up in price or not in the future. Now, you get some insider news that the 1996 corvettes will be going up in prices in 6 months from now. Just like anyone in the interest of making some profits, you start looking for a 1996 corvette, and lo and behold, you find the perfect example of one for sale.

Now, it will cost you $20,000 to buy one, and you only have $5,000 to spare. But you do know that you will be getting a bonus in 6 months for $20,000 which will cover the cost of the car, but unfortunately, it will be too late by then as the prices will go up. So, what you do is this: offer the seller $5,000 as a down payment for the car. You will tell the seller that you will have the full amount of $20,000 in 6 months from now for the car. Until then, you will take the car off the market and in 6 months you will buy it for a fixed price of $20,000. If you can't fulfill the cost of the car in the six months' time, the seller keeps the vehicle and the $5,000, and if you do have the funds ready in 6 months, you can buy the car for the fixed price of $20,000.

Let's now talk about how this would work in the stock trading market. For example, if a stock is trading at $10 and you think it will go up to $20, what you can do is buy $15 "call option" for $0.10. If your predictions were right and the stock did go up to $20, then you could buy the stock at $15 even if the stock is at $20 netting you a profit of $4.90. But like in the analogy above, there is a time limit. So let us say the stock didn't go up until $20 by the time you had predicted it to go up, then you are out $ 0.10 and the seller keeps the $0.10.

Put options

Now, we will be using the same analogy for the put option as we did for the call option. So, let us say you ended up buying the Corvette for $20,000. To keep yourself and the car safe, you decide to buy insurance at $1,000 for a year's coverage. In case of an accident or theft, the insurance company will cover your losses. Let's just say a year goes by and nothing happens to your car. You are happy that nothing happened, and you bought the insurance for your peace of mind and the insurance company is satisfied that nothing happened to your car and they get to keep the $1,000.

In another example, let's say your car has been damaged and it will cost you $4,000 to fix the damages. You decide to use your insurance to cover your losses, and the insurance covers your losses as promised. In the final example, your car gets stolen. Now, you are out $20,000! Don't worry. The coverage is more than happy to cover your loss of $20,000 as it happened within the year. You see, the insurance company doesn't mind paying out $4,000 or $20,000 for your damages when you only paid $1,000 as it is getting the $1,000 premium from multiple people. They would need to pay out $20,000 in that year, but they got $1,000 premium from 100 people, which means they made $80,000 profit in a year.

Now, let's use put option in a trading scenario. So, if a stock is floating around $15 per share and you have a feeling that it will drop down to $10. As a safety net, you could buy a $12.50 put option for $0.10. If the stock drops down to $10, you will still have the possibility of selling it at $12.50 even if the stock is at $10. Netting you a profit of $2.40, on the other hand, this would leave the person at a loss of $2.40 who sold you the "put option." Now, if the stock never drops down to $10 in a certain amount of time and the "put" expires, then the put buyer is out $0.10 and the seller keeps the $0.10 as profit.

It is a gamble.

You are now well-educated on options trading, and you know that it can be a gamble. Therefore, I would not recommend making this your sole income as the cash flow is unpredictable. Exercise this method on the side to make money.

How much money can you make?

Just like stocks, you cannot put a number. People have made millions of dollars from options trading, and some have lost millions of dollars on options trading. So like I said, there is no fixed rate of pay you will be getting, but also, there is no cap on how much you can make.

Now, before you go and try out your luck in this, please remember to know what kind of risk you are putting yourself into. There is no guarantee that you will make money or lose money, it is a gamble. For you to make it less of a chance, find out everything about the stocks you will be buying, know if it will be going down or up in price and then make your call. Just remember to make this your side income stream rather than your sole income as it could lead you to lose some money if not all. So, remember, practice with smaller amounts of money and have the discipline to stop when you feel like you are going into deep.

CONCLUSION

With that note, we come to the conclusion of this book *Dropshipping: How to Make $300/Day Passive Income, Make Money Online from Home with Amazon FBA, Shopify, E-Commerce, Affiliate Marketing, Blogging, Instagram, eBay, Retail Arbitrage, Social Media, and Facebook Advertising.* Remember, the methods in this book, when followed correctly, can yield you amazing results when it comes to making money. However, you need to act on these methods as soon as possible to ensure that you make a great living from it sooner than later.

The last thing you want to do is to procrastinate, that will only hold you back from achieving optimal results. Once you have read and understood the chapter, act on it as soon as possible so you can get going. You will be in a much better position if you act on it as quickly as possible, as compared to waiting for the perfect storm. There will be no ideal time to act on your dreams and goals than now, so make sure you start that business and learn as you go. That is the only way to succeed.

You can read all the books that you want, but if you don't take action, then you will never perfect the skills that allow you to make money. Go ahead and pick a method from this book and start working on it. I am sure that you might fail a couple of times, but eventually, you will succeed. Remember, the difference between a winner and a loser is how many times they have failed. Both have failed, but the one who got back up is the real winner.

DESCRIPTION

In this book entitled *Dropshipping: How to Make $300/Day Passive Income, Make Money Online from Home with Amazon FBA, Shopify, E-Commerce, Affiliate Marketing, Blogging, Instagram, eBay, Retail Arbitrage, Social Media, and Facebook Advertising*, you will find several ways on how to earn money passively while you are at home or doing your daily job. The techniques are explained in detail to ensure readers has understood what they have read about.

Have you always wanted to make money, more specifically, make money while you are in the comfort of your own home, or better yet, traveling? Well, I have a solution for you. In this book, we will show you the top trending ways to make money online and more specifically making money with minimal work. Depending on your goals, you can make $300 a day up to whatever amounts you can think. We say $300 a day because that is the sweet spot for passive income, in this book you will learn.

Introduction: Talk about the book and what the audience should expect to get out of the information provided in this book.

Chapter 1 - The Basics of passive income: Talk about all the new and working methods which will allow you to make money passively

Chapter 2 - Dropshipping-101: Talk about all the ways you can drop-ship such as thru eBay, Shopify, and Amazon.

Chapter 3 - How to be successful when drop-shipping: All the things you need to know in regards to being successful in all the three drop-shipping methods.

Chapter 4 - How to market your drop-shipping store: Talk about Facebook ads, Instagram influences to get sales, and to make money.

Chapter 5 - How to make money from blogging: Talk about a way to make money from blogging, such as utilizing Google ads and affiliate marketing.

Chapter 6 - Blogging 101: The things you need to do to have a successful blog primed to make money.

Chapter 7 - Become a pro-blogger: Which niche to pick, how to write a blog post, and how to market it the right way to make money.

Chapter 8 - Instagram 101: Talk about how to make an Instagram page and grow it to a high following.

Chapter 9 - How to make money from your Instagram page: Talk about affiliate marketing and promotions you can do to make money from this page.

Chapter 10 -Future of passive income: Talk about the future of making money online and passively, allowing you to see what will work in the years to come when it comes to making money.

As you can see, this book is packed with information, allowing you to make money online with minimal effort. More specifically, proving you with the right information, and giving you the tools to make your business profitable from the get-go. Look, we get it. You have been way too tired of spending your time living your life on someone else's term. 9 to 5 jobs aren't for everyone, so if you are tired of living a life in a cage, then you need to get this book now before it isn't accessible to you. If you want to change your life for the good, you need to take action now and make your dreams come true. Now, stop reading the description and start reading this book now! Then go live your life on your terms.

www.ingramcontent.com/pod-product-compliance
Lightning Source LLC
Chambersburg PA
CBHW071504210326
41597CB00018B/2683